NaMo50 to New India

NaMo50 to New India
w/ AGED BANKS

VVSS PRASAD

Notion Press

Old No. 38, New No. 6
McNichols Road, Chetpet
Chennai - 600 031

First Published by Notion Press 2018
Copyright © VVSS Prasad 2018
All Rights Reserved.

ISBN 978-1-948372-35-0

This book has been published with all reasonable efforts taken to make the material error-free after the consent of the author. No part of this book shall be used, reproduced in any manner whatsoever without written permission from the author, except in the case of brief quotations embodied in critical articles and reviews.

The Author of this book is solely responsible and liable for its content including but not limited to the views, representations, descriptions, statements, information, opinions and references ["Content"]. The Content of this book shall not constitute or be construed or deemed to reflect the opinion or expression of the Publisher or Editor. Neither the Publisher nor Editor endorse or approve the Content of this book or guarantee the reliability, accuracy or completeness of the Content published herein and do not make any representations or warranties of any kind, express or implied, including but not limited to the implied warranties of merchantability, fitness for a particular purpose. The Publisher and Editor shall not be liable whatsoever for any errors, omissions, whether such errors or omissions result from negligence, accident, or any other cause or claims for loss or damages of any kind, including without limitation, indirect or consequential loss or damage arising out of use, inability to use, or about the reliability, accuracy or sufficiency of the information contained in this book.

DISCLAIMER

The content of this book is purely personal opinion of author based on his own cognitive and wisdom out of his academic and professional experience over the time.

This book can not be formed or quoted authority at any stages. The facts/numerical data, wherever, referenced in this book are only approximate values and projected only after thorough analysis of various reports published by third party, the government, non government institutes or electronic media etc. The source of the data have been mentioned in bibliography Whenever exact data is printed in this book.

Here in this book if any negative critics embraced against any specific system failure is authors personal opinion. Author strongly believes that single man nor any single institute never make any wonder for considerable period in this mass populated world. Wherein the collective and holistic approach in synchronous only brings the significant positive change in this world. Therefore, distanced himself in criticizing any individual or institute alone.

Every query will surely be attended with highest diligence. However, the delay in the reply should not be attributed to negligence, it is only due to time constrains to the author and his team members.

With your blessing and your cooperation with valuable ideas in making India as New India.

*This book is dedicated to my inspiration
who believes the India as his religion, his cast, his identity,
his strength and all*

*We all call him proudly
As a Missile man of India…,
People's President of India…*

Late Dr. APJ Abdul Kalam.
(1931–2015)

CONTENTS

Preface   *xi*

PART – I
NaMo-50   3

PART – II
Re-Engineering For a Corruption-Free and Cashless New India   37

PART – III
Pillars for New India   75

PART – IV
New India   100

Annexure: One India One Currency One Payment System (IPay)   *123*
Bibliography   *141*

PREFACE

I was stuck penniless and need to travel on vary next day of "Demonetisation day" on 08th Nov 16. The shock is not fully died down yet, After few days many new concepts emerged like Cashless Economy, Digital India, and finally New India. These word seems to be great on plank, but how effectively influence and transform the ground level is under question. May be like you, I also believe in finding the root cause rather than quick fix. These thoughts and hence, work for improvement of our own society translated to form this book in pursuit of sharing with you all.

Portrayed the times of demonetization struggle, effectiveness of present Multi-Payment system, banking infrastructure, AADHAAR effectiveness and magic figures of GDP numbers etc,

After decoding and analysis of these issues, new concept is emerged On new slogans

"One India One Currency One Payment System."

"Universal Basic Income/Investment"

This certainly becomes the thrust in the realization of the dreams of youth, women, farmer, old age and disabled. Proposed methods potentially zeros the suicides of the feeding god (farmer) and youth. Which consequently worth to be called as the New India.

I am sure that Your journey through this book (total parts: four) grabs your hand for participation. Since this book at every stage makes the relevance to your life and your exposure to social & economic conditions around. Hence seeks yours participation by sharing valuable comments and thoughts.

NaMo 50: Two young couple takes you tour through all phases of the demonetisation and its impact on the society and common people around you. They also need your participation in figuring out exact problems and their root Maker. Ironically, They believe banking system could be vital in tuning India into corruption-free and consequently developed country. You only judge their claim.

Re-engineering of System: I mind you that as exactly as you think, *"young and energetic people, yet responsible never leave the problems to continue."* They have shown absolute resistance to the patch work and passive measure in response to the emerging problems. Ohh, they are too tech savvy, they worked towards the re-engineering of the basic personal finance and retail banking system in the backdrop of the AADHAAR, network banking, uses of under utilized postal network. They seek complete makeover of these to have new set up to stand competent for ages. They believe AADHAAR is a hug gift for India, however, voice against AADHAAR Number based transaction by saying "Over-usage of anything results in counter production."

Pillars for New India: Some times, few invented theories are logically flawless, but on application they remains to be ineffective. They have identified few fellow pillar groups whose development is necessary to call any country as developed. For the application of their theories they studied there pillar group core problem with the help of your valuable inputs.

New India Achieved: They applied all theories successful towards the development of those group of people so called as the pillars of the country. Their conviction towards the constitutional right "right to equality" is quiet differs with what other thinks. They claim that equality is constitutionally provisioned but not ensured even after 7 decades of the Independence. This duo promising real equality across India with their theories and some of supporting statistics. Even they stepped ahead of making Development Progress report by ruling government mandatory progress card for the voter on the line "*if the LKG gets the progress card then why not for the voter.*" You just explore and hope your hand joins theirs in transforming India as the NEW INDIA.

Annexture, One Indian One Currency One Payment (IPay) and its software architecture is provided for interested.

Proud to share that the concise form of this book was sent to PM office exactly one year before. It was really encouraging for any one if acknowledgement reaches within one week.

It is absolutely unfitting if there is no mention of the people who worked in reaching your sacred hands in the form of book. Those list is exhaustive but needs mention in honour. First of all I should be grateful to the my organization and people who are around me for more than 15 years. Since they facilitated lot for learning, put high technology in front, provided means to tour around country. Which altogether makes me more and more mature in this world. Another group being the family members, their support only eased my work. Great chunk may be for you too, friends from various sectors from banks, law, and media have the profound contribution. I should also thank Notion press publishing and editing team to keep my interests always intact.

Now as a reader you are new companion of my journey.

I am privileged to feel convenient whenever you contacts for any issues covered in my work

With all of your blessings,

(VVSS Prasad)
M.Sc (EC), MBA (Gen), CDM.
vvssprasad@outlook.com

PART – I

NAMO-50

I hope you were also in shock at least for a while, the moment the wave of demonetisation struck. Hardly anyone knew why this step was taken, how it was implemented and what would be the impact on us. Am I right?

Let's have a clear idea about demonetisation in concise words. It means the act of removing the legal status from the physical currency notes or coins in the country. Exactly this was done on the evening of 08 Nov 2016. The legal value was removed from the existing Rs. 500 and Rs. 1000 currency notes in India.

Though, this is not the first time the world has seen such a step, everybody still panicked. In the past, demonetisation was exercised by countries for various reasons.

Few countries succeeded in achieving the intended goal of demonetisation while few fell short of it. Actually various situations in the country forced us to demonetize currency. For example, high inflation, black money, funding to anti-social institutes, counterfeit currency and in general the goal was to combat financial corruption.

These goals can be achieved by replacing the previous notes with new ones of the same denomination or a different denomination. On rare occasions, all the old notes may be replaced completely with new ones as in the case of the European union. In 1999, fourteen member countries of the European union demonetised their respective currencies and replaced it with the euro, a common currency for all countries. The prime reason for this move was ease of trade between the member countries.

Another successful demonetisation happened in 2015 when the Australian government moved to eliminate counterfeit currency in their country, replacing its currency with polymer bank notes. This led to Australia being the first county to have its full currency circulation in polymer bank notes. Polymer notes are comparatively harder, waterproof, lasts longer and it is very difficult to counterfeit.

In India we cannot blame any single cause for demonetisation. This led to demonetisation, as India, being a rapidly growing country is already preoccupied with all sorts of problems at the highest level. Corruption, financial crimes like fake currency circulation and the black money market, have caused an unfavorable and unstable business environment. A volatile business environment stems the growth of any country and with a greatly diverse country like India, achieving consistent growth would be a long term challenge if these issues aren't dealt with in a systematic manner. In order to address the above problem, the government of India announced the removal of Rs. 500 and Rs. 1000 currency notes from circulation and urged all citizens to surrender the same to the banks within 50 days. The Prime minister of India, Shri *Na*rendra *Mo*di promised an improvement after 50 days and sought the cooperation of all the affected citizens of India of India.

You will journey through this book through two friends who first met on a bus in the vicinity of the port city of Vishakhapatnam around the same time the PM of India announced this historic move. One hails from a humble village background, while the other is from a rich and metropolitan background. This difference in their backgrounds ensures they have opposing views on demonetisation. This duo narrates the various struggles they have faced and heard of as their journey goes on. They also try to formulate unique solutions for the problems faced by the citizens post the move. Now they present these ideas for you to appraise and add your suggestions too.

On 08th Nov 16, after a gap of nearly 6 months, I visited my brother's house at Vishakhapatnam. At the time, he was employed in one of the Indian banks. After I spent some valuable time with my brother I headed back to my native village. At around 08:30 in the night, my brother saw me off at a nearby bus station. I boarded the bus and found an empty seat next to a girl. I was hesitant to sit next to her, but then I thought of the two-hour-long journey in the company of a good-looking girl and asked her, "Sorry to trouble you, would you mind if I take this seat?"

Without any response she quickly adjusted herself to far end of the seat. I thanked her and settled in for the long journey. Soon I pulled out my low-end smartphone with my slow 2G connection and tried to open WhatsApp. While I was waiting for WhatsApp to load, at about 9:30 at night, I received a call from my father in panic questioning me, "How much money do you have in your wallet?" and asked me to draw more money from an ATM or borrow as much as possible from my brother. I asked immediately, "Why you are you asking me to withdraw such huge amounts in such a panicked manner? Is everything okay at home, father?"

"Everything is okay at home but all the ATMs and Banks are going to remain shut for next two days as Rs. 500 and Rs. 1000 rupees are banned from today, by midnight. Our Prime Minister announced this in a breaking news story at 9 tonight," replied my father.

I had just boarded the bus back home and there was no way I could carry out both of his requests. The lengthy journey ahead and this new development plunged me into deep thoughts. I could not look out the window, as the girl sitting next to me kept rocking back-and-forth in rhythm with the bus. All the while she was buried in her premium Apple iPhone.

Curiosity got the best of me and I peeked at what the girl was reading on her iPhone. It was a breaking news story on demonetisation and I wondered why she wasn't upset like me.

Without warning she looked at me with a smile and I felt may be this would be a good time to start a conversation. So, I asked quietly, "Do you have enough liquid cash to complete the rest of the journey?"

With a grin she replied, "I have enough money ... but in my account. Did you ask me this because of demonetisation?"

I responded saying, "Yes that's right. What might be your good name?"

The girl: My name is Adya, what is your name?

Me: My name is V-square S-Square or VVSS as everybody calls me, but my name is VVSS Prasad.

Adya: That's a very strange and lengthy name. I'll stick to VVSS as well, if that's okay with you?

VVSS: Of course, you may. But tell me how are you not worried with the news?

Adya: I think it is a great move and since I don't carry hard currency of such high denominations I am not so worried. I have never felt the need of having too much hard cash so far.

VVSS: Nice! So how do you pay for your everyday affairs? I bet you need to have hard cash for groceries?

Adya: I normally buy from hyper-markets and always pay with my card.

VVSS: Oh! Great, so you do not use hard cash for your day-to-day expenses?

Adya: Yes, I use hard cash very rarely these days. I have multiple bank accounts and their debit cards and credit cards give me a total credit limit of Rs. 5 lakhs. In addition, they give me bonuses every time I swipe my card.

Meanwhile, the conductor shouted from somewhere in the crowded bus, "Please have sufficient change as we will not be accepting Rs. 500 and Rs. 1000 notes to purchase tickets."

When he approached us we asked him, if these notes are invalid from midnight, we still have 2 hours left.

"Why are you implementing it now?"

The conductor immediately replied, "Knowing that these notes are invalid, everyone will pay using the same. Then how can I give out change for so many people paying with Rs. 500 and Rs. 1000 notes?"

While I was patting my pockets for my wallet, Adya had already purchased a single ticket by tendering the exact change. In a couple of minutes, I too asked for a single ticket by offering a Rs. 500 note. To my surprise, he refused the money with a firm question, "Didn't you hear my announcement?" He then demanded the exact change for the bus ticket as well.

On hearing this, I started patting my pockets again, looking for change. I managed to gather Rs. 74, but I was short by Rs. 2 now. I remembered my friend giving me some, which I had tucked into one of the wallet's inner compartments. I found it and paid the exact amount for the single ticket and sat back down with a smile.

VVSS: How did you manage to pay the entire amount exactly in change, when you mentioned earlier that you only use plastic money?

Adya: My mother asked me to carry sufficient change, as she knew I hardly keep hard cash in my wallet. I heard the conductor say something to you, I hope you were able to pay for your ticket?

VVSS: Yes, I managed. The crazy conductor took all the change I had with me, including a relic Rs. 2 note gifted by my friend and kept safe for many years in my wallet. Perhaps he was collecting change so that he can submit all his personal Rs. 500 and Rs. 1000 notes to the bus department after his duty. I blame the sudden demonetisation announcement by the government that led to all this confusion. No one had the time to financially prepare.

Adya: You should understand that, if everyone intentionally pays the conductor
(smiling) the banned notes at a time for the small ticket amount, how can he manage to tender out exact change? I think it was a fair move by him. By the way, your reaction suggests you don't support the move the government made?

VVSS: Yes, I am deeply distressed. I have two lengthy journeys in the next couple of days.

It is foolish as it is and troublesome to the rest of us who rarely visit the bank and barely use e-payment systems in their lives.

I think, you support this move as it barely affects you with your series of plastic cards and multiple bank accounts.

This shouldn't be any trouble for you, right?

Adya: Yes, I support this wholeheartedly and have the confidence that this will not affect my daily life.

Either way, you should have asked me if you did not have enough change at your disposal. So tell me, do you have enough money for the rest of the journey and it slipped my mind to ask you where you were going?

VVSS: I am going to *Mutcherla* village. It is located nearly 11 Kilometers away from the Gajapathinagaram (Gajapathinagaram is a small town in the state of Andhra Pradesh, India). How about you, where are you going?

Adya: I am also going to Gajapathinagaram and I know the place well. Don't you have to catch another bus or an auto to reach your village? Do you have enough money for that last leg of your journey? Let me help you by lending you some money for it?

VVSS: I do have over Rs. 10,000 with me. However, it is all in the banned notes.

Thank you for your offer. Firstly, tell me how you plan to manage your day-to-day simple affairs with your plastic cards from various bank accounts from tomorrow onwards? I ask this since all ATMs and banks are going to remain shut for the next two days and I am curious how you will manage.

By the way, I don't need any money for the last leg of my journey as autos or buses run that route only between 5 pm and 6 pm in the evening.

Adya: Oh, apart from my cards, I have another payment system through my mobile.

VVSS: Through your mobile? How does that work?

Adya: These days I use mobile payments more frequently for all my payments than plastic cards. I have many e-wallets and online banking services available in my mobile.

So tell me, how will you reach home with no transportation facility available for the last leg of your journey?

VVSS: My father will pick me up on his two-wheeler.

Adya: Why would you disturb your poor old father? Especially in the dark when its most dangerous with improper roads.

VVSS: Yes. It is the only way for me when I want to reach my village after 6 o'clock in the evening.

The conductor began screaming out the name of the next bus stop, so that the concerned passengers could get ready in time to get out of the bus with their luggage.

Adya: Have you spoken to your father? Is he on his way to pick you up??

VVSS: Yes, I did. But my call never went through. It could be bad network coverage at my place.

Meanwhile Bus slows down with the conductor screaming at the passengers to get off the bus quickly. The two of us got off the bus as well.

Adya: Have you tried reaching out to him again?

VVSS: Yes. The call should go through now, hopefully.

Adya: Oh great! That's some network you have got at your village!

If the call doesn't go through, it's alright, you can stay at my place for the night and leave tomorrow.

VVSS looked at her with a little smile while waiting for his call to be answered by his father.

The call was briefly answered until it was cut off again by bad reception. Enough time for VVSS to hear his father say that, he was on his way to pick him up.

VVSS: Thank you for inviting me home, but my father is on his way to pick me up. I need to wait for half an hour for my father's arrival. You don't need to stay and wait with me. Your mother may be awaiting you with sweets and warm food.

Adya: (smiling) I have WhatsApped my mother about me being late. I can keep you company you till your father arrives. Let me use this time to get to know you.

VVSS: Have you thought of how wonderful the smart-phone era is?

Some relationships have ended without knowing the names of their partners even after long hours of conversations. I will give you an example. When I asked you permission to sit next to you in the bus, you just adjusted yourself, without even looking at me due to your deep indulgence in your smart phone. Had that phone not been in your hand, you might have had the time to acknowledge me verbally. Am I right?

Adya: Yes, you are right. Before the smart-phone era, people were a lot more courteous to each other. Initially the meeting is always filled with the light process of mutual introduction and then its followed by other discussions. But in the smart phone era this action takes place after the meeting and that too only if both have common interest.

It's amazing how it reduces the distance between sole-mates staying far away and in the other end, increases the distance among the people under one roof to a great extent. However, I was reading the news on demonetisation and it certainly got my eyes glued to the phone. Therefore, I didn't reply when you spoke to me. Sorry about that.

You barely talk about yourself though.

VVSS: I am a simple person with very little education and I hail from a fairly poor village. But you don't appear to have the same background as me. What's your story like?

Adya: I did B.Tech in computer science and an MBA. Since completion of my MBA last year, I am working as an HR Manager in an IT company in Secunderabad. But my native place is Gajapathinagaram and my parents are staying here as well. Currently I live alone in Secunderabad.

I could not come home for Diwali as I wasn't sanctioned leave. That makes it 8 months since I came last.

VVSS: You are as beautiful on the inside, as you are outside and brilliant too. This has been a very special experience for me so far and thanks to you, I have forgotten all the drama caused by demonetisation as well. This reminds me of a famous saying from a famous man.

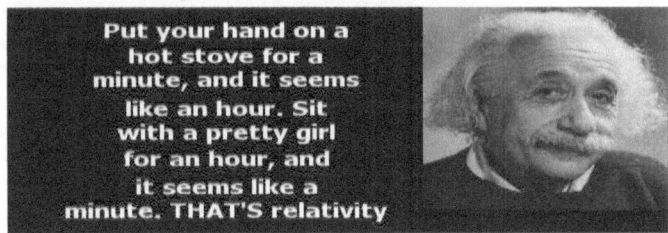

Two and a half hours with you, felt like a few minutes.

Adya: This is too much. Please don't say anything more.

VVSS: It is rare to find a person who has beauty, brilliance and a kind manner.

Oh God! I have forgotten to purchase medicine for my father. I have to find a medical shop that would be open now. I don't want to bother you with this so, you go home and we shall meet again soon.

Adya: It's no problem. I will come with you.

VVSS: We must say thanks to the concept of ATM by Apollo pharmacy. Anytime medicine 24*7 days.

We entered the store and purchased the prescribed medicine and were billed an amount of Rs. 800. I handed out two Rs. 500 note for payment. In reply he said, "We have been instructed by our company that with immediate effect, no Rs. 500 and Rs. 1000 notes should be taken."

We argued that the rule was only in effect from midnight and that there was time. We even tried to convince him by threatening him with a complaint to his company's head office regarding his customer service. We had to resort to every option to get the medicine. Finally, he accepted and gave back change as well.

Getting the change was a big relief! And I said, "This will not work from tomorrow. It's going to be a struggle to get change for my daily needs."

I asked her again if she agreed that demonetisation was a wrong step. Having little education and coming from a village I was struggling. What of the people who are worse off than I am? God can only save them for the next 50 days. Is this your demonetisation? I wanted to ask her.

Meanwhile, my father had arrived which was confirmed over a call. I politely asked her to leave for home now.

Adya: Alright. I will leave after meeting your father. I am going to be here for the next one week. Whenever you come to the city call me. Let's meet?

VVSS: Sure. I feel privileged to have a brilliant girl like you accompany me when I come to the city next. Let's get in touch over WhatsApp. I don't have your number for that though.

Adya: Take my WhatsApp number so that you can be in touch. Now that you have your medicine and change for your expenses tomorrow you can finally sleep well, without thinking about demonetisation. We'll talk more when we meet next. I too had a great time with you. Good night and take care.

VVSS: Good night and take care. See you soon.

We reached home at around 12:30 am, shockingly a lot of small group meetings were visible throughout the village. After lot of strenuous physical work at farm fields throughout the day. Probably, all the discussions and fuss would be around, 'How to convert their money to legally low denomination notes as banks and ATMS are shut the following day?'

I had delicious dinner at home and went on to sleep thinking all about demonetisation, despite my new friend's advice. Despite the low speed internet in the village, I could successfully send a message to Adya, letting her know I reached home safe.

Adya: Good morning. How are you? What did you do today?

VVSS: Today has been full of new experiences.

I woke up at 8 in the morning and went outside the house to catch some sun in these demonetised times. As expected, everybody is clueless about what to do with the banned notes. By this time every one's at work or doing their daily chores. But today they are crowded in front of my house. My dad is well known in the village and they have come seeking answers.

One woman, in her late fifties may be, walked up to me and handed over a roll of Rs. 500 notes. She was crying saying that this was her savings for any medical emergencies that she thinks her alcoholic husband might impose on her. I was shocked at her money management and her responsible foresight.

Even I never thought of keeping money for medical emergencies. However, I assured her that her money would be safely converted. I further, advised her to visit the nearby bank and deposit it or convert it to new notes with a voter ID card or *Aadhaar card for proof. She replied with more sadness that she doesn't even have an account nor has she ever visited a bank in her life. She didn't know how to write her name so how could she visit the bank? She left my house, perhaps, thinking about how to reach a bank she has never seen.

Adya: Yes. Villagers, illiterates and senior citizens were most affected by this move. I agree with you; however, this move will be recorded in Indian history as a symbol.

VVSS: At 9 o'clock in the morning, my parents and I left home to head to the railway station located around the 10 km away.

Adya: That is risky. How could you take your parents on a bike?

VVSS: Hahaha I parked my helicopter on my roof-top and I was robbed last night.

Only available transportation is auto, those were in line at my village auto-stand. But auto only leaves after getting minimum 15 passengers. Is that not risky?

Adya: Oh my God! 15 passengers in an auto?

VVSS: Yes. Regardless, we reached the railway station where the ticket counter was heavily crowded, compared to my previous experience at this station.

---

* AADHHAR: It is an Online verifiable12 digit unique-identity number issued to all Indian residents based on their biometric and demographic data. The data is collected by the Unique Identification Authority of India (UIDAI), a statutory authority established in January 2009 by the Government of India, under the Ministry of Electronics and Information Technology, under the provisions of the AADHAAR (Targeted Delivery of Financial and other Subsidies, benefits and services) Act, 2016.

As the line to the counter was thinning, one person comes up to me asking to exchange his Rs. 1000. I refused to do so as I barely had enough change for our tickets. He requested repeatedly in vain. Again, I convinced him that I could not help him as my ticket's price is very low and the ticket seller would not accept this note. Anyway, I reached to counter to purchase the ticket with my 500 rupees. Ticket seller replied with, "No Rs. 500 and Rs. 1000 rupees."

I said, "Railway stations are authorised to accept the banned notes as per government orders." His instant response was that the government has not sent any new notes to them so they can't accept my notes. They also didn't accept card payments and required exact change for the journey. Despite being the second largest organisation, with more than 1.4 million employees and average annual customers rate is just below the world's largest organization, China state grid corporation. None of the railway station ticket booking counters are equipped with POS or any other e-payment facilities so far.

This is really upsetting that the central government has demonetized the economy and the country's biggest transportation system is not equipped with e-payment options. Tell me what you think.

I finally purchased tickets to Rayagada. It is one of the main city, in the state of the Odissa, India. We are waiting at platform 2 for the train to arrive. The only conversation that I can hear around me is about demonetisation.

Adya: Smile. Just smile.

VVSS: The coach was really crowded and I was trying to find seats at least for my parents. Two young guys respectfully gave their seats to my parents and they joined me at the corridor of that coach. Already a few of them, both young and old, were debating the pros and cons of this move.

Meanwhile, I heard a voice from the group saying something and calling me. "Sir!"

I turned my head and asked, "What?"

"Sir, where are you from? We all got on at the same stop last night, sir. Let's all chat since we are together."

"Tell us what the topic you are discussing."

They said "*Manchi Debba Kottadau Modi Garu...*" (Shri Modi has nicely hammered us by removing the Rs. 500 and 1000 notes). I joined them to get a clear idea on what others thought of the sudden demonetisation and to see if they are supporting it like Adya.

I eagerly asked them, "Whom has he hit?"

They responded, "The bloody money-laundering contractor is being hammered. So far, these people have been leeching off our sweat and they have a lavish life. It is not due to their hard work, but they know the art of the sucking the life out of the poor and helpless. Even government does not listen to our problems. A few government employees also do the same."

I asked, "Who are these people?"

"Contractors, Police, Villagers and other govt administration."

"Here comes another culprit on this list."

"Who?"

"This train ticket collector."

"What happened?"

"He ruthlessly empties all of the money from the wallets of the poor for silly reasons. Poor people cannot afford any other transport means as the rest are expensive."

"I have travelled all across India in the last thirteen years. I personally believe, a majority of the staff in government offices are the most corrupt. However, it cannot be possible that all are corrupt."

They responded, "Yes. Not all are corrupt. There are 20 to 30 percent honest people in every office trying to do some sincere work."

One of them shared his own experience. Every day he is supposed to be given Rs. 250 as daily wage. But he only gets Rs. 200. We have total team of 70–80 members per day, which means the sub-contractor makes Rs. 3500 a day apart from his salary. On questioning him about the reduced payments, they threatened to remove the daily wage. There is no other work available near my village so nobody fights with him.

Now all of these earnings will be deposited to banks or he will lose it all.

Soon the train halted at my destination, Rayagada railway station.

We reached the temple in an autorickshaw. The darshan was very smooth and quick. This was due to fewer pilgrims, which was a result of the demonetisation and fear of travelling with banned notes. Hopefully it would be better in next couple of days after the things settled. We returned to the station, three hours earlier than our trains departure to Visakhapatnam.

We were too hungry as we hardly ate breakfast. We could not find any good restaurant at the railway station or near to it. When we did find one, there was a board outside that stated displayed Rs. 500 and Rs. 1000 were not accepted there.

We needed to have sufficient cash in low denomination notes before having the meal. We enquired about a hotel that accepted e-payment. We walked another 1 km to reach it. Where we saw that 2 percent extra was levied on card payment and Rs. 500 and Rs. 1000 notes were not accepted there.

After boarding the train at the right time, we settled down to sleep. On arrival, we took the bike and started to our village.

We reached home finally and slept after eating curd rice. We got up at the 8 o'clock.

Adya: What's the plan for the day?

VVSS: I have to submit my cousin's college fees and book a gas cylinder.

Adya: How you planning to pay?

VVSS: I will try to pay in either old notes or with debit card if they accept or ask for more time.

Adya: Let's finish the work and then go for a movie or to a park.

VVSS: Okay.

We faced the same issue at the college and were given 30 days extra without any fine.

Adya: Don't worry everything will settle sooner or later and there will be transparency in every business.

What is our next destination? Gas booking right? Do you have money? They will not accept e-payments too. But they do accept the banned notes according to the government rules.

VVSS: Thank God. Let's move.

While we are passing the government utility payment point the queue was overwhelming. Then Adya told me that the government allowed everyone to pay all utility bills in banned notes for the next couple of days. This is a big relief for the middle class and poor people.

Adya: Why are you laughing?

VVSS: Here is another window provided by the government for the brokers and the corrupt. Again people's comfort is of prime importance for petrol pumps and I can understand this situation. Let's move I will show you how defaulters are lined up with their money.

We reached the gas booking station and we noticed a lot of rush exactly as expected. One of the broker asked us to give the money to him so that he can book the gas for me. We said that we have old notes with us for booking. Then he left and faced another drama at the booking counter for the remaining change.

We were finally done with our work for the day and took the bike from the parking lot. On our way, we met with an accident and I took her to a clinic where they refused to take our banned notes again and Adya paid by cash. This is a bad situation for anyone including defaulters.

Adya: I agree hospitals are a black money marketplace due to insufficient and inefficient management.

VVSS: Leave everything here, we will head to your house where you can rest.

We went home and had lunch, while watching the news on demonetisation, a few panelists stated that real estate is going to be a big loser and that market will fall.

I asked Adya how the market would fall.

Adya: For anyone buying a plot in city or anywhere, there will be three rates usually mention by property brokers. One market price might be Rs. 3000 rupees per sq. ft., the second government official says it is Rs. 1000 and the third names a price as per his commission, which is 2–3 percent on the total deal amount from both parties. i.e., seller and buyer.

If the plot is 20*40 sq. ft. then the market price is 800*3000 = 24,00,000 lac. The government price is 800*1000 = 800,000 lac.

The broker's commission is at least 2% plus 2% = 4/100 (24,00,000) = 96,000 Indian rupees.

To seal the deal, the buyer needs to pay = 24,00,000 + 48,000 = 2448,000 rupees.

Now, on the successful sale and transfer of the property, the buyer instantly becomes poorer by Rs. 16,48,000 since he paid 3 times the amount. The seller would illegally become richer by Rs. 16,00,000 and the broker richer by Rs. 94,000. Consequently, seller and broker become richer overnight by taking the hard-earned money of the middle class. This is the way real estate prices go up over time as the property changes ownership.

I forgot, there is another loser in this deal, the government.

VVSS: How?

Adya: In this deal, registration fees, stamp duty and other taxes are paid at a rate of Rs. 8 lac and not for Rs. 24 lac. Secondly, both seller and broker would not show their extra earning in their income statement so this becomes black money for the government.

VVSS: I still do not understand how there would be a downfall.

Adya: Well, all their ill-earned money will be pumped into the banking system and drawing it out again is not so easy as there are a lot of restrictions and rules on withdrawal. Therefore, the supply of money to these idiots has been reduced to zero.

VVSS: I don't think your claim will survive once the banned notes are replaced with new notes and put into circulation in next 50 days.

Adya: I don't think they will be able to carry out as usual in the near future.

Your phone is ringing.

VVSS: Yes, my father is calling. May be to ask me to return early as I have a long journey to Ahmedabad. So take care. See you soon.

Adya: Happy journey and keep in touch. I will try to come to the station to see you off.

VVSS: Not necessary. I will call you frequently.

I went home, packed, left for the station and boarded the train at 12:30 pm. Adya called and wished me a happy journey since she couldn't make it in person. I told her I would call her in the morning.

Thanks to my employer, I was able to travel all over India. Since my younger days, I believed in two famous quotes.

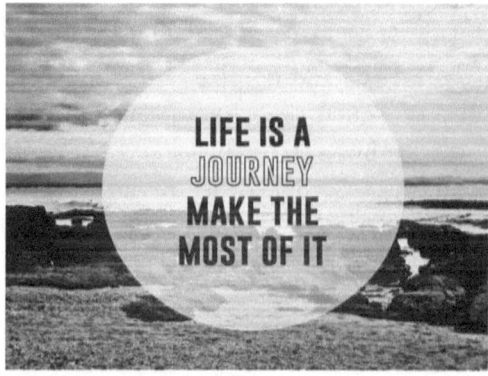

I had many experiences on my journeys and I looked forward to new ones thanks to demonetisation.

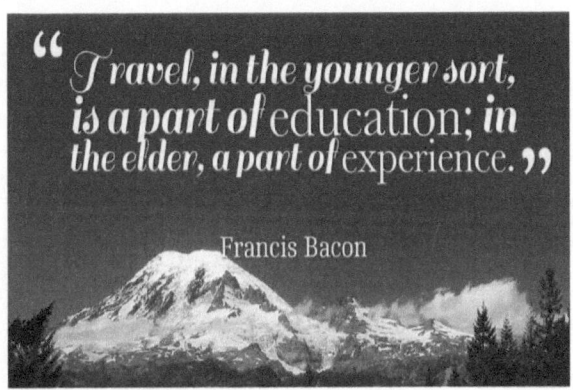

When I woke up I called Adya and enquired about her injuries from our accident.

Adya: Hello! Good morning. I have been waiting for your call since 6 o'clock.

VVSS: Sorry I woke up late. How are your injuries?

Adya: A little painful when I move around. I have extended my leave by a week.

VVSS: I hope you recover by then. I read an article on how the scraping of high value notes would reduce human trafficking, terror funding, fake currency circulation and Maoist activities.

Or its just paid news justifying the move. What do you say?

Adya: Yes, I read it too. Don't over think about the news you read and about whether it is paid or motivated by outside forces. If that's the case, we can never read anything on the news.

VVSS: So you're saying you believe whatever they print and say? Please explain your logic.

Adya: How could anybody manage their business before demonetisation despite having e-transaction facilities and the banking system?

Did you know that hard currency exchange in large quantities used to be common before 08 November 2016? It is because its movement cannot be traced by anyone, so they can hoard the money in unaccounted places and send some funds regularly to anti-social groups.

Since the high denomination notes were suddenly made illegal, their hoarded wealth has no value.

Take the case of the terrorists, for him to enter any country his prime need is hard currency.

Another area is human trafficking. The sheer intricacy and size of the network ensures it is a large industry. This is where people, mostly women and children, are kidnapped, sold or scammed into prostitution or other similar activities by traffickers for their own profit.

Hard currency's movement cannot be tracked specially in high denominations, as is required in this large illegal trafficking network. All this cash is invalid and of zero value.

Another example is printing of fake currency.

Fake currency is put into circulation at ration shops and other rural businesses, and it is very hard for poor and illiterate people to identify these notes. Money collected through this channel is diverted for funding of terror and human trafficking activities.

The new currency has an enhanced unique security feature to hamper the copying and printing of the same. Now they will never be able to acquire the technology which can replicate the new notes as per the claim of the RBI. It is the sole authority for issuing currency in India.

I feel very sad for the helpless poor and innocent people.

VVSS: Your argument is quite convincing, but tell me how long these positive effects will last? I think this effect is temporary. The replacement of currency is rapidly taking place. Do you agree with me?

Adya: Yes and no.

VVSS: What is your answer?

Adya: What you say may take place but it will never be the same as before demonetisation.

VVSS: Why? Once the new money is printed and circulated, everyone can go back to their old ways.

Adya:	They cannot since all the money is being pumped into the banking system and new currency is also coming through the banking system. The accountability of each account is being scanned by the Income Tax Department. Every penny will be accounted for reducing the risk of the same thing happening again. Remember that if you transact more than Rs. 50,000, you need to specify your PAN (Permanent Account Number).
VVSS:	Okay the train has reached the station. I'll talk to you when I get home. Bye!

"It is proven that all our problems emerged because of the aged Indian banking and payment system."

Banks are built in in such a way that it can change the entire country's economic profile or in some-cases world profile. Everyone witnessed this, in the case of the global financial crisis which took place in 2008. This situation arose mainly due to the fall of the banking system in various countries, in which millions of the people lost wealth, jobs and many more. Everybody should accept the fact that banks are vital institutions in any society as they significantly contribute to the growth of the economy through the facilitation of business. They uplift of the citizens of the country.

You have probably come across the word "cash flow" while reading newspapers. Economy is nothing but a combination of various business and their theirs cash flows. Cash flow is the lifeline of the economy. This is a simplified statement. Cash flow in any country's economy mainly happens through the banking system. In order to make the economy grow, an appropriate cash flow must be maintained. The cash flow in the Indian economy is full of leaks, obstructions or disappearances due to illegal hoarding of the money.

After finishing his work, VVSS called Adya.

Adya:	Good evening. You got home early today.
VVSS:	No, I left work early as I have a slight headache, but more importantly I want to talk to you.
Adya:	Oh, what is that important?
VVSS:	I have some thoughts on our long discussions. As per as my opinion, banking is going to play a big role in the future in restricting illegal activities.
Adya:	Oh! Now it makes sense as to why you have a headache, you are thinking about all of this. But tell me has the headache reduced? Have you had dinner or not?

VVSS:	No, not yet. But let me tell you my opinions and plans first. You are well-qualified and have good exposure to the digital and banking system.
Adya:	Alright. Tell me.
VVSS:	The Indian banking system and the RBI do not want to become transparent or user-friendly, though technology has progressed so much.
Adya:	Now you are blaming the banking system?
VVSS:	Yes, absolutely.

Had the banking system been transparent, corruption-proof and more user-friendly, this demonetisation would have been successful or not even featured in Indian history.

Adya:	How?
VVSS:	I have 10 points which clearly prove the laziness of the banking system when it comes to embracing prevailing technology. Whatever technology is being used by banks is being done in a very passive mode.

The passive approach means acting on issues after they have taken place. In other words, they put a solution in place after the problem has already arisen.

A proactive approach means acting to counter any unforeseen eventualities. This is like vaccinating a child.

Adya:	Oh good, you have a better understanding of the word passive. Okay, tell me what your ten points are.
VVSS:	My first point is a lack of customer data integrity and unequal functional standards in the banking system.
Adya:	What is customer data integrity?
VVSS:	Data integrity is the overall completeness, accuracy and consistency of information of the customer across the organisation, here the banking sector. Due to functional loopholes and external admin loopholes one can hold various identity cards with data that does not match. Now they can have various accounts at various places with various identity cards.
Adya:	What is the problem if one has various accounts at various banks?
VVSS:	This is not a problem if the integrity of your identity is maintained. This means all accounts are opened with uniform customer data standards.
Adya:	What is this uniform customer data standards?

VVSS:	Account opening standards are not uniform across all banking sectors. Therefore, many corrupt people are able to hold various accounts and even proxy accounts with the help of different kinds of identity proof. This facilitates the hoarding of their ill-earned money, which will never be traceable.
Adya:	No, this is not possible as these identity proofs are only given after the verification of their identities.
VVSS:	Wait, my dear! I will explain!

Various banks have different rules, even the various branches of the same bank have different rules in establishing identity and address verification standards for bank account opening.

It is a well-known fact that these identity cards can be easily procured in multiples in India.

As I frequently travel across India, a few genuine banking branches insist on at least two kinds of identity proof to establish your identity, but they need only copies of any identity proof to open an account.

So, it is very evident that if one opens accounts at various branches with his multiple identity cards to mislead a third party that enforces rules and regulations. It is only detected if the case becomes very serious and comes into the public eye.

Adya:	You wanted to prove that various identity cards of a person shows the person as multiple individuals.
VVSS:	Yes, but not always. I am only concerned by the ill at heart. Just take the case of my own identity. Some of my identity documents have my complete name whereas a few do not my third or second name.
Adya:	Okay agreed. Tell me the remaining points.
VVSS:	The conservative approach to the poor class and the aggressive to the elite class
Adya:	You mean to say that banking is discriminating against the poor?
VVSS:	Absolutely right.
Adya:	Is it in some explicit way? Each class has various banking needs. A businessman carries out huge transactions and has time constraints. Banks cater to different section of people with different approaches and different facilities.
VVSS:	Yes yes, I will tell you one small story I found on Facebook.

At one of the bank branches, an old lady handed over a cheque to the bank teller and said, "I would like to withdraw Rs. 500."

The female teller told her, "For withdrawals less than Rs. 5000, use the ATM available outside, please don't waste my time."

The old lady asked, "Why?"

The teller irritably told her, "These are the rules. Please leave if there is nothing else, there are a lot of people waiting behind you."

The old lady remained silent for a while and asked the teller, "Please help me withdraw all the money in the account."

The teller was astonished as the lady's bank balance was 3.5 billion rupees. She politely told the old lady, "Our bank never has dealt with such a huge amount of cash. Currently, you can withdraw up to Rs. 300,000."

The lady said, "Okay, please withdraw Rs. 3,00,000."

The teller gave her the amount.

The lady then said, "Please deposit back Rs. 2,99,500 in my account."

This shocked the teller some more.

What a management principle you have too. You are saying that banks should formulate their own conduct according to the elite. I agree with you but why not the same with poor customers.

In India banking conduct in such a way that just lavishly sanctioning the public funds to corrupt business peoples in thousands of crores without even basic verification. And struggling to get that amount repaied. But for the poor farmer and student aspiring to do business, they have to make hundreds of trips to the banks to get the credit of the sub-lack level money.

You know one thing that they are not only serving lavishly business but also at low level disbursement funds in unjustified way take the example of agri-loans to few elite personnel who never farmed even perhaps seen the farm land in their life. Just aggregate these outstanding dues to banks is going to be shocking figure for everyone.

Adya: It means, with aggressive and lavish lending to elite class increases the NPAs in banking sector, in turn availability of credit to true citizens are restricted, in my opinion.

VVSS: What is this NPA?

Adya: NPA means Non- Performing Assets. These assets owned by banks and gets no returns over the time as these assets (amount) are given to customers in the form of loan for interest but banks failed to recover the principal/interest on the loan over the significantly longer period, as a result it remains as not performing in the banks records (no returns on the banker money given to customer).

As per my financial academic terms:

A nonperforming asset (NPA) refers to a classification for loans on the books of financial institutions that are in default or are in arrears on scheduled payments of principal or interest. In most cases, debt is classified as nonperforming when loan payments have not been made for a period of 90 days.

VVSS: Thanks.

Adya: It is okay but explain the remaining portion. Conservative banking to poor.

VVSS: The banking system does not include the poor in their plans. They believe they will never get significant business from these people. Poor people will not make substantial deposits in banks. Consequently, the banks do not invest in resources to offer them good services and credit. Thus reducing the liquidity of these areas. This leaves villages with little or sometimes no access to banks and their facilities.

Adya: But these days, do you know that, the maximum amount of business is happening with these people.

VVSS: This is due to the government's proactive policies, not the banks.

Adya: What are they?

VVSS: Look at Janadana Yojana Accounts, the opening of a large number of these accounts across India happened through the government. Agri-insurance, a few state government schemes like in Andhra Pradesh, the DWAKRA groups which mandate groups to manage every paisa through the banking system. The business of banking is spiking due to the demonetisation drive as these accounts have been used as *Benami* accounts by others for their gains, that is for the exchange of old notes.

Finally, what is the need of the government along with the RBI to announce the exchange of money at any branch without any need of account. Since the banking system is out of reach of the common man, this fact is well known to the government so to reduce the trouble for the common man they have placed this rule.

Adya: But this is for a small amount perday. That is 4000 so it is minute. Do you feel that this becomes a good gap for the big money change? I doubt it.

VVSS: Yes, this is the primary window miscreants found. I will narrate an experience, which I forgot to share earlier. When I visited the bank for withdrawing money by cheque. There was a big rush, nearly hundreds were queued up. While I was writing the cheque at the writing desk, one young illiterate person came to me and requested furnish money exchange performa.

While I was furnishing it, he was scolding his contractor. I enquired why he was scolding him. In response he said, "I, along with many, have been standing here to exchange his money since early morning."

Just imagine if he has 50 daily wage labourers then he can very easily exchange 50*4000 = 200,0000 per day.

More importantly, these people block the way to the bank counter for the honest poor man and ease the way for the contractor to exchange his money. Consequently, the sufferers are the poor and middle class.

Definitely this could not have been able to find it place in this era of technology, if the banking facility was available to the common man.

What do you say?

Adya: Quite an interesting revelation.

VVSS: No, it is not an allegation. It is true. Don't you realise by looking at previous experiences in you recent past?

Adya: What is your next point?

VVSS: Passive and slow approach to the problems with the technology by RBI and major banks, especially government banks

Adya: That's a confusing sentence.

VVSS: It sounds like that. Banks usually facilitate the services according to problems that prevailed or employed technology already used by some other players. This may not be their peers but it is definitely being used by similar institutes in sometimes, the same industry.

For example, the RBI introduced NEFT technology in 2005 for all the banks. However only private, premier banks utilised it. The government banks took several years to catch up with this trend.

I faced this personally when I opened a bank account with HDFC and they could offer me NEFT transactions. But my public bank could not do this.

Another fine example is the BHIM app, though well-designed and efforts have been made to facilitate modern payments methods like QR code and mobile number-based payments, however, it is a passive measure. Private platforms like Paytm were already in place long before BHIM was rolled out to the public.

Adya: BHIM shows their passiveness when it comes to addressing problems.

VVSS: Poor infrastructure and facilities for poor man and also for the middle class in some areas.

Adya: They don't discriminate against customers based on financial status.

VVSS: Do you live in India or a foreign county?

Adya: Why do you ask this?

VVSS: Poor men have to stand in line often for hours after traveling long distances from their villages. But rich hardly need to visit the branch and if they do they get better and quicker facilities.

Secondly, in cities you will find streets full of banks. But in villages like mine, people like me must travel a minimum of 10 km to find a basic banking facility.

Adya: Yes, I have heard how the banks treat villagers like you.

VVSS: Poor mobile payment, online banking system and customer support by the banks.

Adya: Most of the banks offer internet payments and mobile payments. What is the problem with you?

VVSS: If the mobile and internet payments were so effective, then why did so many people struggle post the introduction of demonetisation?

Do you think these banking payment systems reach all the people in the country? SBI mobile banking, have come up new version of the android app that lacks basic functionality. The app size if big so you must possess a high-end smartphone and even then, it is very sluggish to use.

Adya: I agree that customer care is not good on any of these facilities.

VVSS: Yes, it is quite pathetic.

In July 2014, I was pickpocketed while boarding a bus in New Delhi. While I was wondering where to find alternative money, my mobile received an SMS from SBI (State Bank of India), saying that a penalty of Rs. 15 was deducted from my account due to an incorrect withdrawal attempt. I made a call to customer care and asked about the ATM address where my ATM card was used by the thief. Customer care refused to give the information saying that we will provide it to the investigating authority if you file a complaint. Had the customer care provided the information I would have reached the spot with the help of the Delhi cop. And do you think they are good enough to cater the low or illiterate people in such instances?

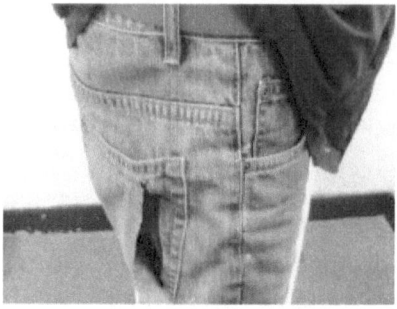

Adya: But tell me your opinion since I am in such a frenzy about Paytm. Since everything is brought under one roof such as shopping, recharge of various services, mobile DTH, travelling service and also supports payments for online purchases and for offline purchases at markets with small vendors. It is an easy way to pay without any requirement of POS machines. Anybody can pay for his purchases with his smart phone just by scanning a QR code. They challenged all other payment systems with their innovative way of business. Right! Do you agree?

VVSS: Yes, of course it has challenged many banking and non-banking payment systems by using contemporary technology in an optimum way.

Paytm, despite being an innovative payment system and its' unique style of business, can it ever be the main payment system in India?

Paytm is also being misused greatly by various departments due to poor banking and money management in India.

Adya: My favourite payment system also comes under your criticism, it is okay. But tell me more about its' misuse during demonetisation.

VVSS: I will give you a personal observation of when a customer tried to pay via Paytm. When I asked the mobile number or QR code for the Paytm wallet, the shopkeeper replied that they had overshot their limit on all the wallets available.

Then customer asked what this was.

The Paytm wallet limit is only Rs. 20,000 per month per wallet. I have totally 8 wallets fully filled with customer payments accounts. These accounts include 4 of my workers Paytm wallets. I don't have a problem since I have been making all of my payments even on amount higher than Rs. 20,000. The shopkeeper replied that in order to extend the limit I needed to compile the KYC norms. And furthermore, they needed to give me only 1 lakh rupees of limit. In that case, how am I benefited?

I thought initially that he was right but while walking away from his shop the actual cause of non-compliance was ascertained.

Adya: What is that?

VVSS: If he compiled the KYC norms for him and his family members then his limit would have been increased to 8 lakhs instead of the current 160,000 per month. There is another reason for not compiling the KYC norms and that is mainly due to the accounting and hence, taxation problems. He is not providing any bill to any one and he sells the goods to various people at different prices according to his wishes. Therefore, he has to fill the income tax returns and officially carry out the wallet business of 96 lakhs per year.

Apart from this, they face another burden of transaction charges levied by Paytm for the high amount of transfers. That too, the transfer amount takes different time frames to reflect in the account statement. Now tell me, is this good and convincing for medium and higher business entities to maintain this as their sole payment system?

Adya: I never thought of it this way as my payments do not amount to so much. Essentially you are stating that Paytm cannot be the sole payment system in India?

VVSS: Yes, but one should not rule out the pioneers that they are. They have encouraged the government to think more innovatively. Perhaps the BHIM payment app is inspired by Paytm.

Adya: Why couldn't the Indian banks produce this system earlier? It would have been useful for honest customers and businesses.

VVSS: This is my next point.

Banks heavily rely on third party payment system providers like Visa, Master Card, Maestro and recently RuPay by the National Payment Corporation of India.

The responsibility of the continuous development of these payment systems fully rests with these companies. These third-party payment services play mediator between the customer and the bank.

FEW OF LEADING BANK MOBILE APPS

- These pictures themselves narrates full story about "how poorly managed digital User Interface" by leading banks.
- Does it confusing for customers or not? If one needs to handle e-ways for financial transactions, he must be be Tech-Savvy means he should have fair knowledge of technology.
- Current banking system really failed in crafting digital platform with simplicity, transparent and user convenient Digital User Interface.
- With these many limitation and flaws, how one can expect these services to be expanded successfully to all corners of India.

VVSS:	Banks will also be puzzled if they see these screenshots.
Adya:	Maybe.
VVSS:	You are quite knowledgeable about these things and have associated with many financial and IT firms yet you are confused too. What about the simple man? Definitely he should be an IT engineer to understand and use these apps. Am I right?
Adya:	Alright. But why are banks not doing a good job on this front?
VVSS:	Staffing.
Adya:	Yes, you mentioned this at the end of the last call. Tell me how the staff at banks are the drawback for growth on the digital front.
VVSS:	They adopt a conventional recruitment process and do not recruit as per the demands of their business model, especially government banks.
Adya:	What does this mean?
VVSS:	How did you get your job? There must be people already working in your company for years that can do your job but instead of placing them in your position, how did they choose you?
Adya:	I understand your intention. Banks should carry out campus recruitment.
VVSS:	If necessary, but they should recruit suitable talent persons according to the needs of the position and the market. The scope of talent and innovation is restricted right now.

They should let eligible employees from within the company compete with outside talent for the same post to ensure it is fair.

You cannot expect the old, conservative generation to manage the next generation. This can only be possible with the involvement of the current generation.

Adya:	You mean to say that the new generation alone can address all our problems?
VVSS:	No, you misunderstood. The previous generation must have the assistance of the responsible and smart young generation to make any organisation innovative. The recruitment policy should be created accordingly to serve our enormous, diversified nation.

To help you understand my view, let's discuss two of the most prominent personalities in India that are making waves with their talent and skills. One is Sundar Pichai, CEO of Google and the second is Arundhati Bhattacharya, CEO of SBI (recently retired).

Adya: Yes, both are great personalities. What is your problem with them?

VVSS: I have no problem with them. They are a huge inspiration to the entire world. I would like to compare these organisations and how these talented people have been used by their respective companies.

Adya: What aspects of comparison?

VVSS: Sundar Pichai took only 10–11 years to become head of one of the world's largest tech companies whereas Arundhati Bhattacharya took 36 years to do the same in India. She put almost her entire work life into the same organisation, beat gender issues, bore the extra responsibility of family life and the burden of organization internal politics.

Pichai does not have a degree in computer science. He did his B.Tech in Metallurgical Science as well as an M.Sc. and MBA. Despite this, he heads the software giant where thousands of IT professionals already work including those that are experienced. This is smart recruitment by the company's top brass.

Adya: You mean that Arundhati Bhattacharya is not that talented. You know she was declared one of the 25 most powerful women in the world.

VVSS: Hold your breath for a moment. I think you, being girl are much inclined to her in this debate. If she were not the head of this India bank, it would have been in a miserable state by this point as said by many insiders. It would have been struggling to survive in this technologically-rich society. Due to her administration capabilities the organisation has survived at least, thanks to the way it has handled technology and the low-class customers.

Adya: What do you mean?

VVSS: Take a second to think first. Listen carefully to everything I have to say or you will hammer me.

Adya: I just think what you are saying is odd.

VVSS: I am not blaming her for this delay of 36 years to climb to this position. I am absolutely blaming the organisation for missing the opportunity to utilise her talent to its full potential at an early stage due to its outdated recruitment policy.

If their recruitment policy was like Google's or Microsoft then she would have been at this level much before 36 years of service.

Adya: What I understood from your explanation is that large organisations should have different recruitment policies to hunt for hidden talent no matter where it can be found instead of sticking to their conventional policy of only picking people from the senior staff of the organisation.

VVSS: Exactly. Sometimes, an outside observer has a better understanding of the situation and can handle it effectively if control is handed over to him.

Adya: What is the next point?

VVSS: No one has done any monumental restructuring of the banking sector. They always do patch work when the problem overwhelms them.

Adya: What is this?

VVSS: It is nothing but the restructuring of the current organisational set-up at a fundamental level to suit the prevailing economic, social and technological challenges.

> *"Fundamental rethinking and radical redesign of business processes to achieve dramatic improvements in critical measures of performance such as cost, service, and speed."*
>
> – Michael Hammer and James Champy, 'Reengineering The Corporation,' 1993

Adya: Explain with an example please.

VVSS: Nokia is a good example. It has fallen from being number one to nowhere in the world.

When technology is advancing towards artificial intelligence but you are still hanging onto the old OS, one must try to make things newer.

Due to demonetisation and the emergence of the new concept of a cashless economy, every bank has recently started working to streamline their apps to ensure the customer feels comfortable managing his banking transactions with smartphones. However, this is also seems to be patch work and not a complete revamp of the payment system.

Adya: Yes, they are enhancing their apps with new features and better design after the demonetisation and cashless economy drive by the Indian government.

VVSS: Poor marketing.

Adya: Marketing? Why do banking services require aggressive marketing?

VVSS: Without the proper marketing you cannot sell your goods before their expiry date.

Adya: I agree.

VVSS: Have you ever been approached by a banking executive to promote their banks services or financial products?

Adya: Yes, I do. I was approached by bank employees marketing their credit cards and a vehicle loan.

VVSS: Who was it exactly? Do you remember? Which bank did he represent?

Adya: I cannot recollect his identity but he was from the HDFC bank.

VVSS: Exactly. Due to their aggressive marketing and ease of business, HDFC has lead the credit card market in India for years.

Adya: Okay fine. But why can't they do innovative retail banking?

VVSS: These private banks have good operations in cities and substantial annual growth. They only target premium customers with seamless banking services according to their needs and their convenience. They have nearly 4500 branches but none of these branches is near a village. From my home, I have to travel nearly 35 km see my private banker HDFC.

In order to build a good financial system of the India, nationalized banks should take their services to the poor of the country with a seamless, transparent banking experience. They failed here as per my opinion. Had they included these words in their mission statement, the PM would not have needed to launch Jana Dhana Yojana scheme.

Adya: Do you really feel there is a requirement for more marketing by the banks after the government has publicised these schemes?

VVSS: Yes, absolutely. You have a good smartphone and a cable connection with a variety of channels, so news comes to you quickly.

What about us? We don't even know how a smartphone looks and some villages do not have mobile communication.

Tell me, which media channel do villagers have continuous exposure to?

Adya: Fine, I know only the names and a little about the schemes anyhow.

VVSS: Villages are full of illiterates or primary school drop-outs. They need a through explanation in person or through any other means of marketing to understand and avail the government financial scheme. The government launched a scheme called Fasal Beema (crop insurance) to assure every farmer that the government is with them if their crop yield is reduced due to natural calamities.

A couple of years have passed since its launch and my villagers do not know anything about this scheme.

Adya: The spread of schemes has not taken place due to the absence of technology and banking facilities in poor villages.

VVSS: Marketing is the creation of demand and hence growth.

Adya: It sounds good but what does it actually means.

VVSS: Presently, banks are not able to create demand for their services in a proactive way as they don't have any aggressive marketing. They serve after the creation of demand has been done by a third party. It clearly visible in nationalised banks.

Adya: They are not up to the mark. What is the next point?

VVSS: The banking sector is not considered the backbone of the country's growth by our government since independence. And they also failed to identify it is a tool that could eradicate corruption.

VVSS: In my opinion, the banking system is responsible for the country's growth. It alone changes the fate of the country's economy.

Adya: Why do you say that?

VVSS: Consider if all the earnings of a family are not regularly accounted for and managed properly by the family head causing them to face dire problems.

Extend this principle to the country which has numerous families. Do you see what I mean?

Another example I would like to remember is the recession. One of the main causes in my opinion was the banking system's collapse in major countries. If the entire world is shaken by poor banking systems, do you think that banking is not important enough for a country's economic growth.

A bank is like the circulatory system of the body, if it fails completely the mind, heart and muscles will collapse in seconds. That is the power of the circulatory system of the body.

Adya: Despite the poor banking system, India was not on the receiving end of the recession's impact. As per your claim, India should have collapsed.

VVSS: A good question. The main problem was credit crunch, which was not apparent in our banking as compared to other developed nations since no country does any significant business with our banks. So, no country severely suffers with the collapse of the Indian banking system. We cannot

	deny that we were absolutely unaffected. Anyhow I am not in the mood to turn your attention towards the economy of the country but I want to focus on the banking and payment system.
Adya:	We have faced a lot of problems and also analysed their root causes. But do we have any solution for this and can we personally change this system in India?
VVSS:	Unlike the previous governments since independence, this Indian government is one touch away from the common citizen. There are so many channels of direct communication that have been established by the government to facilitate easy interaction and grievances redressal for the common man with all departments and also to the PM. I sent one project 'IPay' to the PM on the 31st of December 2016 and got an acknowledgment within fifteen days.
Adya:	That's really great. This is the first time I am hearing that a common man got feedback from the PM on sending his suggestion. It implies the PM is keen to listen to the people of India and not only from bureaucrats.

But tell me what did you send to the PM?

VVSS: I will tell you later. Until then guess what it is about. It's time to go to sleep.

PART – II

Re-Engineering For A Corruption-Free And Cashless New India

VVSS: Good morning, Adya.

Adya: Good morning, tell me what you sent to the PM.

VVSS: First tell me, what you have understood so far.

Adya: My understanding so far is that due to demonetisation many problems emerged from banking mismanagement and poor technology handling to provide services to customers. Their mismanagement forced the common man to face several cash problems.

Indian banking is at the core of other hostile issues raised post-demonetisation. This is mainly because banking is continuing to use outdated practices despite technology being available to improve their methods. Here the question arises, is there any quick-fix solution to reduce the technology gap?

> **India has highest bribery rate among 16 Asia Pacific countries: Transparency International**
>
> LUBNA KABLY, TNN
> UPDATED 07 MAR, 2017 12.18 PM IST
>
> MUMBAI: India had the highest bribery rate among the 16 Asia Pacific countries surveyed by Transparency International. Nearly seven in 10 Indians who had accessed public services had paid a bribe. Contrast this with the least corrupt country – Japan, where only 0.2% of the respondents reported paying a bribe.
>
> The only silver lining is that over a half of the respondents from India were positive about the government's efforts to combat bribery. Even as the government's efforts to tackle bribery were appreciated, slightly more than 40% of the respondents viewed that corruption had increased over the past twelve months. 63% of the respondents in India also felt that they as individuals had the power to fight corruption.
>
> The Global Corruption Barometer for the Asia Pacific Region was released by Transparency International (TI) - an anti-corruption global civil society organisation, at the stroke of one minute past midnight on March 7, in Berlin.

VVSS: This is wrong.

Adya: What?

VVSS: No more quick-fix solutions. All patch work done so far has created a complete mess. Whatever solution we introduce in the future should meet the basic criteria of a cashless economy with full-proof transparency and accountability for the long-term. These should be at no extra cost to the customer.

Adya: At no extra cost?

VVSS: Yes, with the available technology, including Aadhaar, whatever reforms are implemented should be cost-cutting bonuses for the banks and the government.

Adya: Do you have a plan?

VVSS: Yes, I have been thinking for a long time about a simple one. I hope we can address many problems including financial irregularities, Benami transaction, reduction in corruption and increased efficiency of the Indian administration. This is my simple formula;

THA

Adya: What is THA? It is funny that your simple three-letter word is the solution for a wide range problems and corruption.

VVSS: It is certainly a magical word. I will explain.

THA

T = H + A

TOTAL ASSETS = WALLET ASSETS + A-VAULT

This is a very simple formula where all (liquid) assets should ideally be in a person's hands (hard cash in wallet) or directly/indirectly linked to A-Vault.

Adya: You mean all assets should be in your A-Vault like a Paytm e-wallet? No bank deposits or any kind of liquid investments. How this can happen?

VVSS: This is not a traditional e-wallet. A-Vault is the personal financial record of every individual citizen.

Adya: I think they already have this data against the PAN number. With the PAN number, they can summarise all your transactions. That is the reason why PAN is mandatory while making high-value transactions and for opening bank accounts. So why make it Aadhaar-based?

VVSS: Yes, I know this. But tell me, why is there still so much financial and bank-related corruption in India?

The reason is simple; one can obtain more than one PAN number but never more than one Aadhaar. I will give you a simple picture here for better understanding.

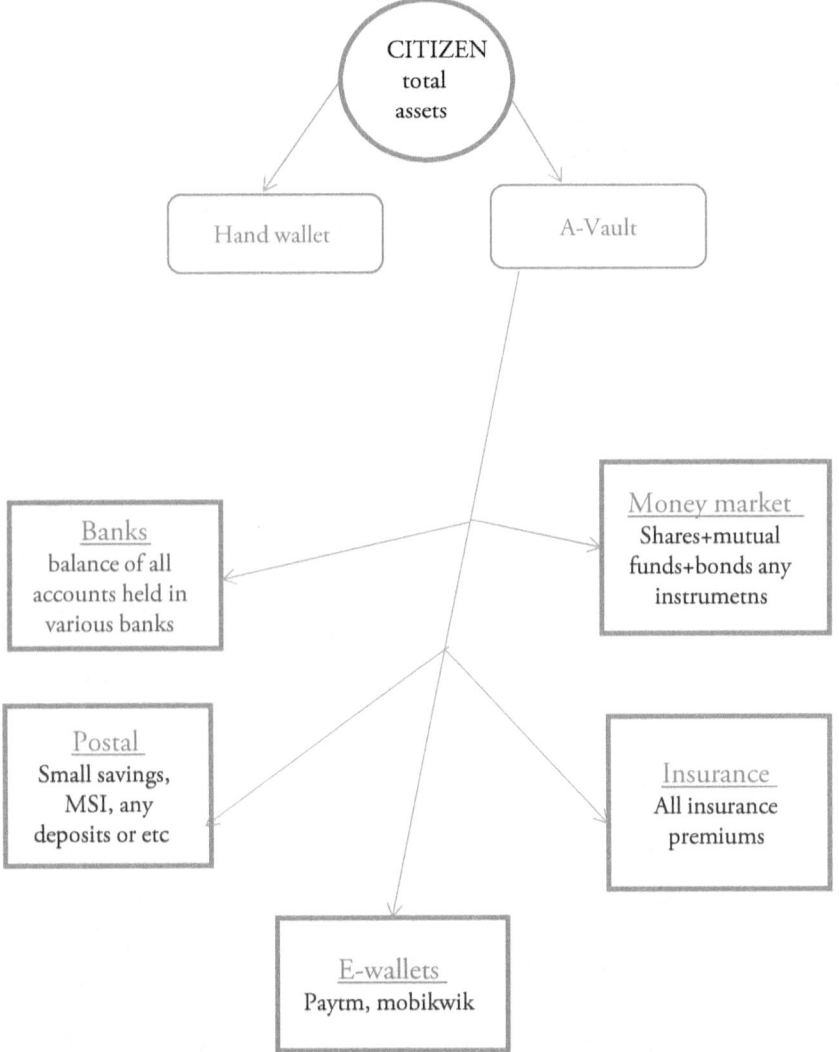

Here one's total assets is equal to the cash in hand plus the assets linked to the A-Vault.

One's earnings are usually kept with the person in hard cash or as deposits in banks for the interest. The main aim of this scheme is to have clear accountability for every citizen's wealth. Due to identity duplication so far, no one could carry out the clean accounting of an individual's wealth. Thanks to Aadhaar, the identity problem is solved.

Whenever someone earns and deposits the amount for interest in banks, the total value of the A-Vault increases and similarly whenever someone uses the money on a luxurious trip then the total value of the A-Vault gets reduces. And if he loses the share values in the market then this Vault balance reduces. This happens as all assets are linked to the Aadhaar number.

This is very useful to track one's financial transactions and assets. It is a win-win situation for honest citizens, the banking system and the government. It eliminates financial irregularities and also equally plays crucial role in the design and administration of the welfare schemes transparently based on the data it generates over the time with respect to each person. Secondly, as the true financial status is on table, we can move gradually towards the economic based reservation or preparation. This is so far never been successful drive for any government.

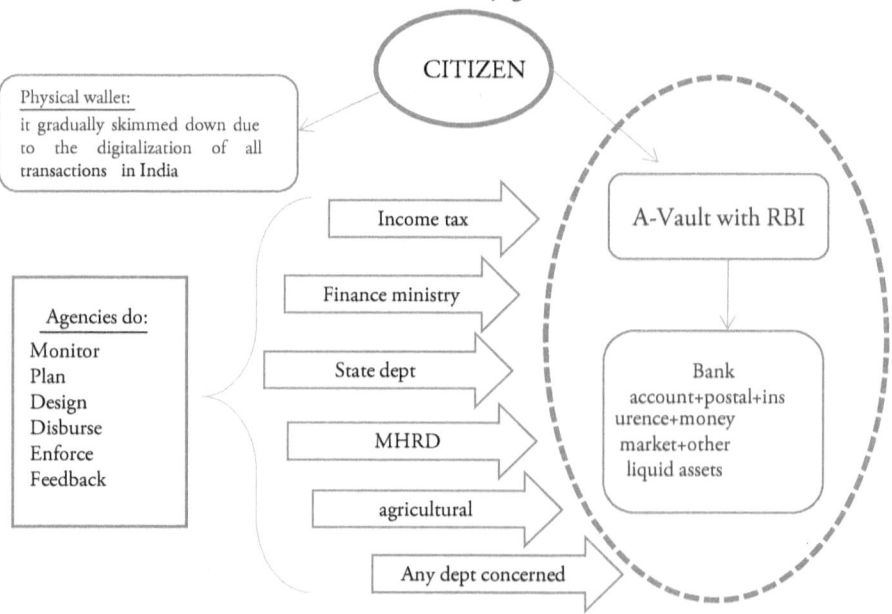

This figure basically explains how the government and other agencies concerned with individual incomes and expenditures and other financial figures, can have access to the database of A-Vault that will be maintained by the RBI. This is not a real-time monitoring facility available to any of the above departments. They all have request-based access to the database on a case-to-case basis. Easy and real-time access to data by departments headed by political entities could lead to the exploitation of data for political gain and sometimes hamper the financial privacy of the individual.

Here is one point worth mentioning, every government strives to provide common facilities to those with a poor financial status in the country.

Adya: Currently government relies on the PAN not the Aadhaar. It still says for high-value goods like gold and land purchases the PAN is mandatory. A few states have started asking for Aadhaar number with PAN number for real estate and recently the government has become strict about linking the PAN number to the Aadhaar for getting Income Tax Returns filed.

Do you think this works for the near future?

"PAN (Permanent Account Number) should see its last days"

VVSS: Yes, I am coming to that point. PAN should have been buried in a graveyard by now. Its framework does not eliminate identity duplicity unlike the Aadhaar.

You know, it has been shocking that the PAN is mandatory henceforth for bank accounts. I saw this in a news report.

> **Mumbai man loses Rs 2 crore online, cops find 108 fake bank accounts**
>
> AHMED ALI, TNN • CITY
> UPDATED 2 HOURS AGO
>
> • The 72-year-old was duped by a Facebook friend with the promise of lucrative profit in an investment scheme in Afghanistan.
>
> • During interrogations, police found the gang had opened fake accounts in various banks in Mumbai and Delhi.
>
> MUMBAI: The cyber crime police probing a Rs 1.97 crore cheating of a Bandra senior citizen by a Nigerian gang have found 108 fictitious accounts opened in various banks in Mumbai using fake PAN. Police have arrested the kingpin of the fake PAN card racket from Naya Nagar in Mira Road and got the bank accounts frozen.
>
> Police said the 72-year-old Bandra resident was duped by a Facebook "friend from the US" with the promise of lucrative profit in an investment scheme in Afghanistan. The investigation led the police to Delhi, where they arrested Mangal Bishnoi, Amit Agarwal, Sameer Merchant alias Karan Sharma, Jitendra Rathod and Paresh Nisband into whose accounts huge money was transferred by the Bandra resident. The money was immediately withdrawn or transferred from these accounts.

Adya: What's the problem?

VVSS: It is problematic and increases the burden of administration. Moreover, Aadhaar is easier to obtain as compared to PAN.

I think the PAN does not have any relevance in the Aadhaar era. Therefore, only one step needs to be taken by the government and the financial department —make the Aadhaar number mandatory instead of the PAN. This means to ask everyone to provide Aadhaar number everywhere, for all banks accounts, all postal accounts, insurance, loans and while availing government schemes.

Adya: Is it possible all of a sudden? I think it is not possible. That is the reason the government is planning to ask every PAN holder to update their Aadhaar number.

VVSS: I think it seems to be using old wine in the new bottle.

Why is the PAN framework needed now? This is like using whitewash before strong weather-proof paint on the walls. All PAN cards are sanitized by linking them with the Aadhaar number and it is an extra burden for the administration.

Adya: Everything sounds great. We have already discussed how the banking infrastructure will never reach every man in this country. All your plans are based and work only if all of Indian citizen use banking and other financial systems in their day-to-day business.

Am I right or not?

"Current banking services in numbers in India"

VVSS: I have the solution but let me tell you some number-based factors with respect to the banking in India. It is prudent to analyse the current statistics before formulating any new plans.

Fact 1: According to the 2011 census of India, 68.84% of Indians (around 833.1 million people) live in 640,867 different villages. More than half the Indian population lives in rural areas.

Fact 2: As on March 31 2015, the total number of banking branches in India stood at nearly 165,000 including commercial (public and private) and rural banks.

Out of these, only 48,000 branches are in villages while there are 6,40,867 villages in India. This means for every 13 villages only one bank branch is available.

Fact 3: According to the latest data released by the Reserve Bank of India and National Payments Corporation of India, the total number of ATMs in India stood at 2,19,637 by the end of December 2016. There are only 40,480 ATMs in rural areas. That's roughly one ATM for sixteen villages.

Nearly 18.5% of the total Indian ATM network is available to the rural population who form 68% of the total population of India.

Adya: That is a large gap between urban and rural banking facilities. These are shocking figures, especially 70 years after independence.

VVSS: Wait, there is another crucial factor. Our country has great diversity in all possible perspectives.

In term of religion, caste, literacy ratio, climate, income, and wealth. We have large differences with any county in the world.

VVSS: This is the only aspect they needed to consider while the banking and financial set-up was planned.

"According to World Bank data, the number of bank branches per 100,000 adults in India was 9 and 13 in 2004 and 2014, respectively. This is broadly in line with the global average of 9.1 and 13.4 branches in 2004 and 2014, respectively.

For ATMs, the Reserve Bank of India (RBI) data say that as of August 2016, there were 202,801. The World Bank data show that the number of ATMs per 100,000 adults in India was 18.07 in 2014. This is way fewer than the global average of 43.9 ATMs."

Whenever I come across such statements, I feel very shocked. We should not be proud of having figures that match the world averages. In 2014, a majority of developed countries were already using smart payment methods like online payment systems. As a result, they hardly need any physical banks and ATMs as per CNBC and other reports,

Belgium is the world number one with the Noncash payments' share of total value of consumer payments: 93 percent Belgium has limited cash payments to 3,000 euro. Punishment for violation attracts penalty up to 225,000 euros.

And if we go mile ahead, world longest street as well as the longest coastal line country, Canada stands at third position with 90 percent.

Starting in February 2013, Canada stopped minting and distributing pennies, supposedly saving the country $11 million a year.

Finally our old rulers United Kingdom stands 4th position in world with 89 percent.

You know one shocking, Before, you step on one of those famous double-decker buses in London, make sure that you have an "Oyster Card" or a prepaid ticket on you. Only 1 percent of commuters used cash in 2014, compared to 25 percent in 2000. Is this possible in india? another, these three countries stand far ahead of India in transparency rating (means low corruption)

Had the RBI and Indian banking system thought of this before 2014, by now the number of ATMs and banks per village would have been better figure compared to the current ratio of 1:16.

Of course, thanks to Janadhana Yojana and direct benefit transfer schemes have picked up pace across India and driven all citizens towards banking services.

Adya: I have heard these schemes enhance financial inclusion. But how can we bridge the infrastructural gap of banking services in India?

VVSS: Without the full-fledged outreach of banking facility to every man, the mission of a cashless economy and therefore a corruption-free India will remain a dream forever.

Initially we can start with a complete cleansing of the existing banking infrastructure and extend the conventional banking system to rural areas.

Adya: What is this cleaning?

VVSS: All banks should clear their accounts system of proxy and duplicate accounts. They should do away with PAN and link all accounts opened with the Aadhaar.

Adya: What about the expansion of banking services to the poor villages?

VVSS: We need to ensure banks are available in nearby cities for banking services. It is highly impossible to extend the current banking system to every corner of India. I personally also do not expect much from this banking system since it is not going to be cost-effective for any bank or the government to expand it.

"True cashless-economy can be realized with mini-banks."

Adya: How can we overcome the banking infrastructural gap between the urban and rural?

VVSS: We need to have mini-banks. They are a little different from conventional banks.

Adya: We need to open mini-banks in every village, but it is a Herculean task since Indian villages do not have a basic infrastructure. What do you think?

VVSS: I have my eye on the post office.

Adya: Post offices? But their duty is to handle the mail service so how can they play a role in banking service?

VVSS: I agree with you. But tell me, how many times have you visited any post office in your life?

Adya: Why do you ask? I have hardly visited the post office after my primary schooling.

VVSS: That is the reason you have such an impression; you need to know a few facts about the post offices in India. Along with mail services, post offices work as small savings banks. They offer the services of Post Office Savings Account, 5-Year Post Office Recurring Deposit Account (RD), Post Office Time Deposit Account (TD), Post Office Monthly Income Scheme Account (MIS), Senior Citizen Savings Scheme (SCSS), 15-year Public Provident Fund Account (PPF), National Savings Certificates (NSC) and Kisan Vikas Patra (KVP).

But all these services are offered with no computing integration like you see in the banking system where all the branches and banks are interconnected.

Another interesting fact is this is the most widely-distributed postal system in the world. As of 31 March, 2015, the Indian Postal Service had 154,939 post offices, of which 139,222 (89.86%) were in rural areas and 15,826 (10.14%) in urban areas. This is an absolute contrast to the Indian banking services.

There are roughly two post offices for every nine villages as compared to two banks for every twenty-six villages. It has comparatively greater reach to the villagers than the urban inhabitants.

Therefore, they have both infrastructure and experience in handling money along with mail services, so let's use their resources in a more optimum way with a little advancement of their services.

Adya: Great, but why this is not coming into the spotlight? Banks are there often. The government should concentrate more on post offices.

VVSS: There are many reasons as per my opinion.

The postal service is under the Department of Posts, which is part of the Ministry of Communications and Information Technology of the Government of India not under the ministry of finance nor under the Reserve bank of India. Secondly, and unfortunately, despite being a part of the Ministry of Communications and

Information Technology, the technological improvement of these post offices has always taken a back seat.

It is in competition with private courier services despite having the largest network. If this postal service had been continuously upgraded with prevailing technology, Indian's postal network would have been the leader of the parcel and mail service sector in India by now.

However, after 2014, it is going in the right direction very slowly.

Adya: What direction?

VVSS: According to the Economic Survey 2015–16, the integration of all 1.55 post offices into a computer network by the end of 2017 with an outlay of Rs. 4,909 crore under the IT Modernisation Project of the Department of Posts was taking place.

Adya: And what else would aid the realisation of mini-banks in villages?

VVSS: There is already a fair post office infrastructure in place in all major villages. So now, the first requirement in turning post office into mini-banks is the set-up of a computer network with connection to the core Indian banking network. This must be done rapidly, so that Indian people can experience the positive effects of demonetisation.

Secondly, the augmentation and training of the postal employees is necessary so the workload can be managed properly.

Thirdly, current post office ATMs also should be on par with ATMs run by banks.

The fourth, all accounts should be linked to Aadhaar numbers.

The fifth one is to extend the post office network to other villages, which eagerly await their own post office.

The sixth being the disbursement of all welfare schemes to villages through mini-banks.

Adya: You are determined to prove that mini-banks are helpful in bringing everyone into banking and achieve the government's ambition of financial inclusion.

VVSS: Yes, this can be achieved. The majority of the Indian rural population has no access to basic banking needs. By turning the already established postal network into mini-banks across all rural areas, we can ensure every citizen can avail true banking services and feel that his earnings are secure. It reduces distance, inconvenience and customer service problems in banking. It is one stop solution to all banking related problems.

Inappropriate and injustice in punishing the common man by banks & government.

Adya: Okay fine, I forgot to tell you that I came across a few interesting news articles in all the newspapers and on social media. They cover various penalties and punishments for over usage of banking services for cash transactions. These further indicate that banks and governments plan to launch more coercive measures to discourage the common man from cash transactions.

VVSS: Stop! Tell me one thing. These coercive measures are going to be enforced on only the poor man or on all Indian residents? Usually punitive measures are equally applicable to all in the country irrespective of their financial, political and social status. So you might have drawn the wrong inference from these news articles. What do you say?

Adya: No, it was a logical conclusion drawn from the news.

VVSS: Tell me the logic behind your blame on banks and the government.

Adya: Presently, the government is demanding every citizen embrace the banking system and subsequently cashless transactions through by introducing e-payment systems at some outlets. On the other hand, the banks are waiting to dip into the pockets of the common and uneducated man.

If you look at the proposed chart of the charges on cash transactions that they are going to implement from the 1st of April 2017, it is evident that banking is deeply in love with the financial elite and reluctantly aligning itself with the government's ambitious cashless economy drive.

Tell me one thing, who transacts more through cash? I am sure only those in the lower middle class and below. Perhaps, senior citizens who do not know how to use an ATM and depend on physical cash for their day-to-day transactions more than any other class. By default, none of this applies to the rich and the upper-middle class.

Who maintains the low-profile accounts? Only the poor and middle-class as they have hardly any money left with them to keep a sufficient amount in the accounts. Besides, bad banking facilities, their poor technical illiteracy adds to the banks bonus. Am I right? You know, they are also charged for e-banking.

But for the elite accounts there no minimum balance with an unlimited number of transactions free of the cost. Banks are running on fees collected from the poor. Since, the rich never need physical cash in huge quantities except on rare occasions thanks to they know how to handle technology and e- banking facilities. But the elite with the wrong intentions who are not willing to contribute a digital payment for the money manipulation can very well capitalise on this provision.

Internet and mobile banking are also chargeable beyond twenty free transactions. For high-value accounts, it is free of cost and unlimited.

In short, the poor and middle class have to pay hefty fees for services at the branch which are not only located miles away from them but also provide poor service. Meanwhile for the elite, everything is free of cost including the esteemed treatment at their nearby branch. How is this fair? I think, the poor are discouraged or virtually expelled from banking services.

This proves the banking sector is against the cashless economy and financial inclusion program. If the elite are punished with charges for frequent and high-value cash transactions then they try to collect their revenue from their respective businesses in e-cash only. Thus, all poor customers will automatically embrace the banking services and e-payment systems.

Take the example of the business entity. If he is charged for frequent and high-value cash transactions, then he automatically asks his customers to pay bills via e-payment which is a contrast to the current trend as businessmen usually insists customers pay in cash.

VVSS: Hold on, madam!

Just observe the table. It is mentioned that deposits above Rs 25,000 are chargeable against the current account. They will not do business with the money; they will insist on e-payments.

Adya: Oh my dear poor friend, your logic seems to match with the banks thinking, but not with my logic.

Since there are fees on high-value deposits, they usually put the money in a hideout or do business with physical cash wherever possible and ensure others accept. He will not lose business as customers are not capable of paying bills electronically.

For example, a hardware shop usually has a turnover above Rs. 50, 000 in semi-urban areas. Customers do not have e-payment facilities on hand. At the end of the day, they will deposit Rs. 25,000 in the banks and the remaining will be stashed or used in other cash transactions. Or else customers would be charged extra for his profit margin so he can cover the bank charges to do clean business.

Secondly, there is no cap and penalty for drawing of the money by the elite people. They absolutely free for whatever the amount they draw and whenever they draw. Even not be humorous if banks said to be their personal money assistants especially hard money.

These kinds of rules are really not aligned with a cashless economy.

The government enacted the law in the 2017 financial bill which states if you carry out transactions anywhere beyond Rs. 2 lakhs in hard cash, it is an illegal and punishable offense. This act was made after recommendations to the Supreme Court by a Special Investigation Team (SIT) on black money.

VVSS: I think your argument is right. However, I have the exception for your claim that it is laid down to discourage miscreants and money launderers from using any huge cash transactions. Secondly, it encourages others to get on the e-platforms for their day-to-day transactions, which consequently enhances the cashless economy.

Adya: We have discussed the efficiency of the current banking infrastructure and operations and how our outdated banking and its payment system cannot reach the poor people.

I strongly believe
"children's behaviour is more influenced by the silent environment
than a louder command…"

I have a classic, real-life example to explain my claim. Tell me what happens if you harshly or kindly tell your kid to behave in a particular disciplined way or to learn something without putting up a sufficient and suitable infrastructure and environment around the child?

In general, everybody thinks it is sufficient if educational classes include well-trained teachers and students. Nowadays, there is no need to send our little kid to school since high-speed internet brings the classes home. Yet, smart parents always verify, scrutinize, shortlist schools after considering hundreds of other factors before enrolling the student.

Can you tell me why they do this?

Parents believe that the appropriate, conductive environment allows students to learn more than the information taught on the blackboard. Here's a simple example, if the movie theatres and a sound-polluted environment is present around the school/college, would you like your child studying there?

It is also applicable to the government and banks. They should build the infrastructure and conductive atmosphere before asking citizen to behave in a particular manner.

Take another example, in one state, one administrator introduced a rule stating it is compulsory to wear the helmet with immediate effect after witnessing multiple accidents. It impacted lower classes badly. They hardly know the new rules and regulations months after the passage of these despite the announcement always appearing in electronic media or newspapers.

The reason for this communication gap is the majority of the poor do not have access to these media. And some never find the time to watch the news due to fatigue following a whole day of intensive farming. Whenever he sets out on any road with his small motorcycle without the helmet then he is harassed and charged hefty fines.

Tell me who suffered more? The poor man riding his bike or the rich driving his car? You know another fact? There were no helmets available across the shops for those who wanted to purchase them. Of course, following a lot of protest the government diluted helmet rules.

Finally, I would like to say that it is unfair and unjust to penalise poor people with hefty fees and legal punishments. Even if it kills the main goal of financial inclusion. It terrified them so much that everyone even tried to draw maximum permissible amount and keep it at home, which is against the cashless drive.

VVSS: What kind of environment do you need?

Do you feel the current multiple payment system can make everyone cashless?

Adya: You have mentioned a good solution—bridging banking problems in rural areas with postal mini-banks in all corners of India. I want to remind you that the proposal alone never produces the realization of the dream. They must be thoroughly implemented.

Secondly, I think after mini-banks you proposed a new payment app under the heading of mini-bank or Indian postal bank. Right?

You have already prepared a lengthy list of payment systems and various payments apps under each bank. This adds to the apps in India which already make people mad. Therefore, we have to find a new alternative solution to the existing payment system for a seamless e-transaction experience for all sections of people in India.

VVSS: Why do you want to add another payment method to the existing multiple e-payment methods like internet banking and banking via mobile app. The government also recently launched its first payment app —BHIM (Bharat Interface for Money—a Mobile App developed by the National Payments Corporation of India (NPCI), based on the Unified Payment Interface (UPI).)

Adya: As per my opinion, payment systems with different procedures are the people's only problem.

> *"Currently, one needs to be tech-savvy to pay e-money securely and utilise multiple vendors."*

Do you think these multiple payment methods can help farmers, students and less literate people to manage their daily banking and financial business in cashless ways?

Take the example of farmers, 90 percent are illiterate. If all expenses should be made through e-payment methods while purchasing the farming-related requirements. Do you think it is possible with the current payment set-up?

Currently, a few farm product traders use various payment systems. Only a few accept hard cash, a few accept debit and credit cards but with the extra charges, a few accept only wallets etc.

In order to have his farm material, he should be tech-savvy and then he may make the 80 percent payment via e-ways. Will this ever be possible for poor and illiterate people?

I am utterly sure that it is nearly impossible for poor and illiterate farmers to do all of their farm purchases in this manner.

This is the problem for other sectors also. The current payment methods are not at all conducive to ever transform this society into a cashless one. There are numerous demerits as compared to their usefulness.

Look at the cumbersome current payment cycle and methods. These discourage a cashless society.

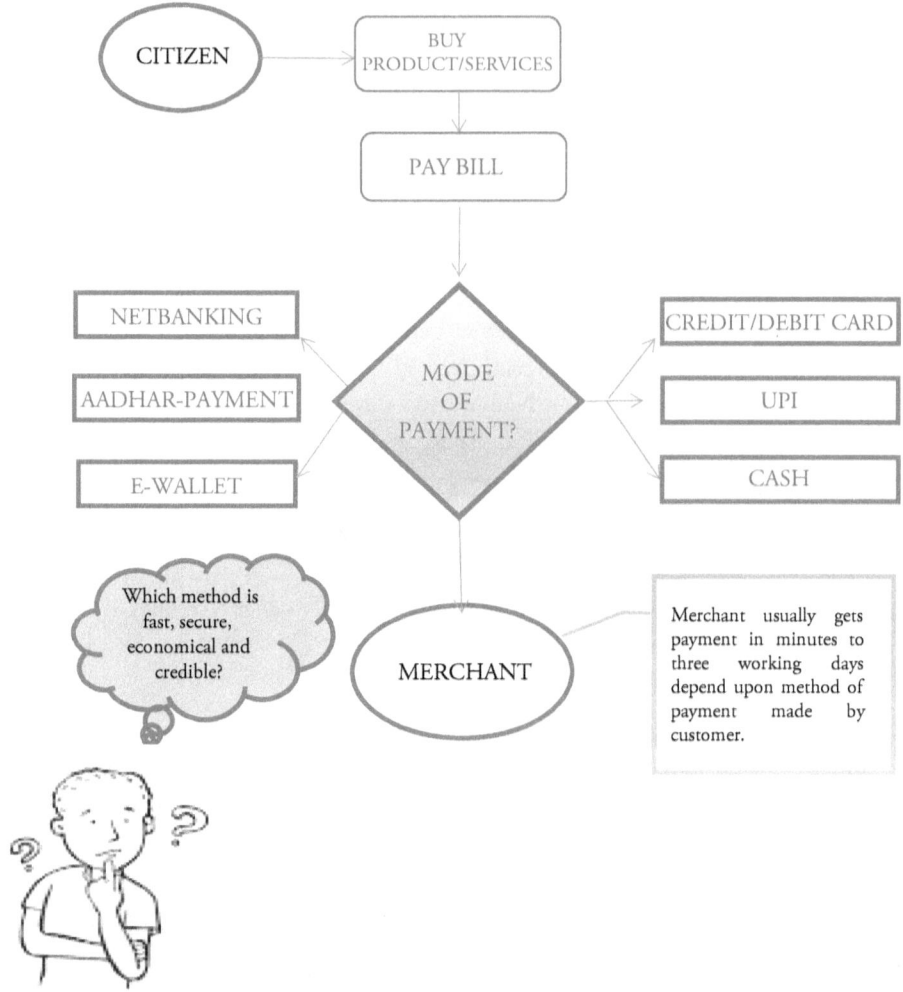

Full Cycle of Payment with Present Payment Methods

Let's start on a positive note. There are numerous digital payment systems in place for the people of India to use. In turn, increasing the flexibility of payment options but there is a parallel reduction in terms of credibility, security and uniqueness to below horizon level.

None of the currently available payment systems will ever be competent enough to serve the entire population of India.

Every day fraudulent transactions take place due to a lack of security and continues because the tracking of transactions with respect to each customer is not in place. This is mainly due to several flaws in our banking system.

Our banking and non-banking institutes have the poorest customer support. Shockingly, the wallet services offered by many companies today are still not able to cover the lower section of urban people since there is no support for services on basic phone models. A few companies do not have easily reachable customer support for quick resolution of disputes. A few wallet services have only email support.

Banks that offer good service will never be within the reach of the poor and the villagers. ATMs, today a basic need of the people, are still not installed in villages or at least near them. The reason behind this discrimination? It is not profitable to banks. In this case, the government has no right to ask people to stock money in banks and carry out digital transactions for everyday payments.

Going for e-payments is costlier and not secure for both payer and payee compared to hard cash transactions. Most payment methods require good smartphones/computers with internet except USSD-based system. Apart from the equipment cost, a user also pays extra for the transaction cost. These can only be used by educated and tech-savvy people not common farmers.

The flow of money takes a longer path in the case of third party wallet usage, therefore the transaction settlement is longer. No real-time settlement occurs (Citizen -> Bank -> Customer Wallet-> Merchant Wallet-> Merchant Bank Account-> Merchant).

Unstructured Supplementary Service Data (USSD), though secure, requires several attempts at dialing and the establishment of a longer connection to complete the transaction. It is a cumbersome procedure.

So far, the government has not exclusively supported/nor recommended any one existing payment system as unique and official. Therefore, a long-term assurance is not there. There may be a chance of fraudulent conduct by any third-party company or part of that company. And nobody must be shocked or even question the existence of the company in business.

There is no compelling law to adopt any unique and fast method of payment for merchants. Even the government cannot enforce the adoption of the current payment system as it has numerous limitations.

VVSS: I agree and extend warm appreciation. You have drawn a logical inference supporting my claim. However, the newly-launched BHIM app has better prospects in comparison to all other apps. Since it has a small size and an easy interface anybody can easily use it. What do you say?

Adya: Yes, it has a good design. Do you know that it is not available for basic phones and more importantly for higher volume transactions? It does not support a few accounts which have old debit cards that do not bear an expiry date. Another aspect is that it has a limitation on fund transactions with respect to the volume that is Rs. 20,000 per day and Rs. 10,000 max. per transaction. Do you think that it can serve your daily transactions easily?

VVSS: For me, this is okay. Since I don't have that many daily transactions. But, I agree with the remaining problems.

Adya: It has not addressed the problem of merchants as well. More importantly, it supports multiple current payment systems.

VVSS: Yes, I agree. We have to produce a unique solution addressing all the shortcomings of the current payment system. The next generation payment platform should be designed to make everyone cashless.

Adya: (smiles) You want to empty all cash with everybody. What is a solution to make everyone use only e-payment systems?

Need of uniform, authentic futuristic e-payment platform from beggar to billionaire

VVSS: Do you agree that the hard currency being used has the same weightage and characteristics in everyone's hands irrespective of their economic, social, political and educational status?

You may be wondering what is the common aspect!

But if you speak about e-money, it has different perspectives with different people. If someone rich wants to handle it, he can carry e-money very safely and transact it everywhere since they have same infrastructure set-up. However, if one poor man wants to use e-money he cannot handle it safely and confidently. Secondly, the right infrastructure is not available around them.

Indeed, it divides people into many categories such as those who use plastic cards, high-tech payment systems like NFC, the second category being wallet users and the other being the poor who do not have any payment system.

Whereas, with hard cash, it does not divide anyone. The transaction cost remains the same, the transaction experience and time remains the same for all and the safety concern is also the same.

When you transact with hard cash, it is universally acceptable. However, e-payments or e-wallets are not being accepted universally.

It makes you poor on somedays for many reasons. It could be the limitation of the payment system you use or the vendor does not accept this form of payment and you need these goods urgently.

Both these cases promote two things, you should receive the same currency type or an e-method which is accepted across India, no matter the volume of transaction without any problems and extra fees.

Do you agree or not?

This is only possible if the existing single paper rupee currency is replaced or becomes a substitute with a unique e-payment solution that involves one and only one payment system across India.

Completely new payment methods should be launched to inspire every citizen to do cashless transactions. My basic aim is to bring about uniformity among all Indians in their e-payment methods as uniform physical cash is being used. This means the 500-rupee note is the same for all and payment systems that matters are the same for all—the poor and the rich.

Adya: What could be this new method? Why is it needed?

VVSS: As everyone knows, cash is the main instrument of exchange for any kind of goods/service purchased. Cash is usually exchanged between the below parties for various reasons whether legal or illegal.

- Man to man,
- Man to business,
- Man to children,
- Business to business (legal or illegal)
- Man to office (legal or illegal)

And places of storage:

- Banks
- Investments
- In houses (legal or illegal)
- Benami savers
- Hideouts

Hey! Do you want to add anymore?

Anyway, initially we discuss the money exchange before the storage of the money. I think so many ideas are taking root in your mind. Right?

The main characteristics of hard cash is that it is uniformly acceptable and guarantees a quicker transaction time.

Currently in India, in all cases, one can do their daily transactions hassle-free and quickly with hard cash. But with all the available e-ways, no one in India can do this, irrespective of whether one has mastered online banking, all kinds of plastic cards and other wallet services.

Do you agree with me or not?

Do you think he can survive all the time with these available e-services as easily as a person who only does the cash transactions?

Certainly not.

Many places do not accept e-cash and only a few places accept e-wallets while others accept only cards.

Secondly, the limitation of services also makes a person poor if he does not know how to carry out the transaction for the remaining amount.

Adya: How can one be poor with the e-payment system?

VVSS: What if you have only an e-wallet on hand and need to pay the merchant Rs. 30,000?

Would you be able to pay him on that day? The maximum amount you can put in an e-wallet is Rs. 20,000 per month.

1 lakh per month if KYC norms compiled.

The second fastest method is the Immediate Payment Service (IMPS). But you cannot send it instantly, though its name claims this since one needs to register their bank details first. In subsequent instances, it may be faster.

This new payment system should become a sole replacement for every legitimate cash exchange in this country without any extra burden like extra fees, difficulty to pay, delay time, need for a high-tech platform, etc. On successful replacement, all illegal exchange of cash is not possible and subsequently at times, illegal transactions tend to go to zero. With the proposed banking system changes, the storage and manipulation of money in legitimate ways is also going to be easy in India.

UNIQUE AND UNIFIED PAYMENT SYSTEM (UUPS)

UUPS is the payment system could be one and only system that caters to all payment needs for all the people of India. In other words, it potentially replaces existing cash transactions from the level of beggars to millionaires gradually. This happens as it would be fully supported and run by the government of India through a central banking and monetary authority, which is the Reserve Bank of India. This payment system is analogue and a replacement for the currently existing Unstructured Supplementary Service Data (USSD) and Aadhaar-based payment system which runs on the Unified Payment Interface (UPI) framework.

Adya: What is the aim of this UPI system?

VVSS: This is a single payment system that becomes a complete substitute everywhere for a single type of currency. There is a uniform transaction time for all unlike the current systems with varied settlement times for various types and volumes of transaction. A feeling of uniqueness among the people of India will arise with the same payment system from the beggar to the elite.

So everyone gets the same experience as with hard cash. This is the most important aspect of the payment system.

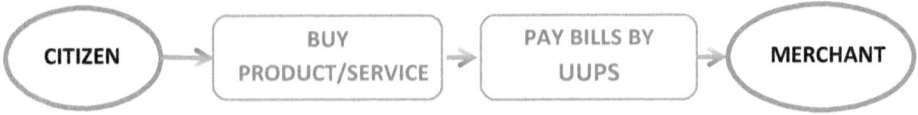

In order to address the shortcoming of the presently available payment system, a new unique and unified payments system, IPay is designed to support the payment needs of all people in all corners of India irrespective of their financial, technical and social status.

I suppose this payment system should exclusively be handled and maintained by the government of India. It will be treated as official Indian digital currency. As a result, embracing to this system is automatic for all Indian people.

The design of this payment system has taken place after a logical analysis. There are five categories of people in India as per their income.

Adya: There are only three types—the rich, middle class and poor. How are you saying there are five categories?

VVSS: Be patient.

There is no official categorisation. I have my own categories and it is not as per the financial statutes.

It is purely based on the reach of technology, affordability and competence to handle it. Though it has been many years since the mobile communication launch, many village do not have mobile towers and even if they are present people cannot afford or handle the devices. Therefore, we should categorize and analyse these before rolling out any new payment method across India.

The first being the group that does not have the basic communication and banking facilities. Perhaps they may not know of their existence like tribal people in remote hill areas.

The second group is the poor, who do know the existence of both and often they avail of minimum services with a basic phone.

The third is above the poor. They use low-end smartphones or hi-tech phones and they often use banking services.

The fourth is those people who have average access to both mobile technology and banking for their day-to-day transactions.

The fifth and final one is the rich. They have every modern technology and banking infrastructure at their feet.

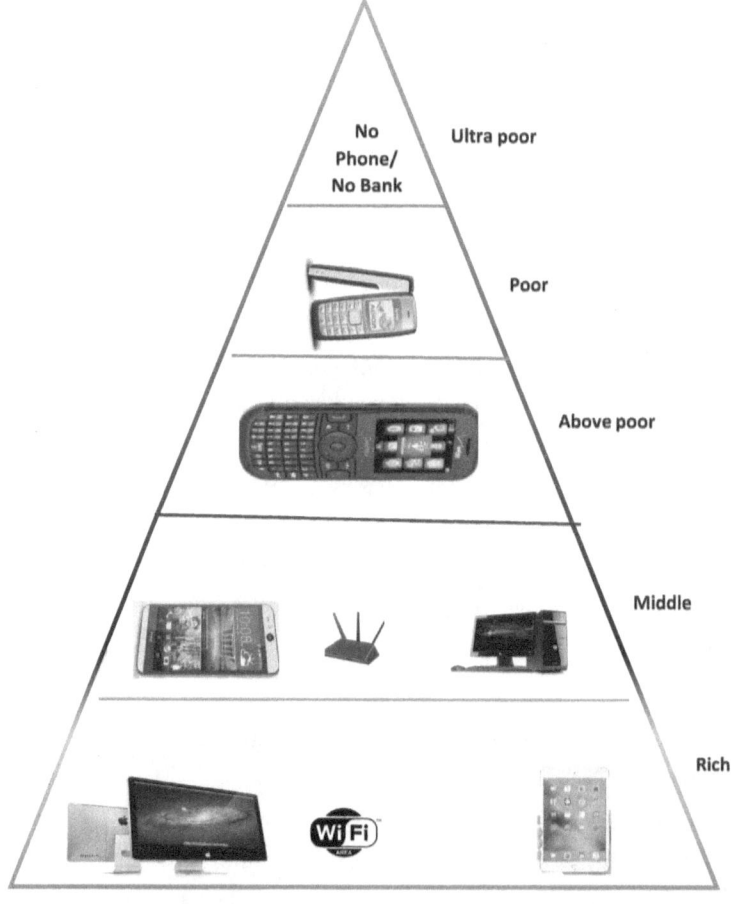

Technology reach pyramid

I feel Indians should be covered by all of the above categories. Of course, if you have any thoughts to add, please let me know.

My aim is to propose a uniform e-payment and transaction experience irrespective of device. This new payment system will address all the problems so far.

This new payment system is named IPay.

You may ask why IPay was coined.

It means: I (ndia)-Pay (ment System).

If you have a better idea for a name, please propose it and we will shift to that name.

"Ipay framework and its detailed working methods are given in Annexure and Online for your reference. All valuable comments at every step are looked diligently, so that improvement can be made in the next book with your name annotated next to the amendment you made"

One should be in the driver's seat always

Adya: After the set-up of a well architected payment system, how can the illiterate and those with a poor understanding of technology be driven towards these new facilities in the villages.

VVSS: A very important question. It is going to be a big task for us. I have a few ideas. Just see if they will work out or not?

Adya: What are they?

VVSS: I should mention that the usage of banking services increased manifold over the past five years for many reasons. However, not being used consistently by the customers. The reasons being, you know better.

The reasons why everyone preferred hard cash over the electronic methods is low faith in technology, guidance and customer care and a lack of awareness of the benefits.

There three kinds of people in India:

One who uses banking facilities regularly in any of the available ways. As these people are well-educated. Usually they do not need service though they bear any kind of interface or another kind of complexity in accessing services.

The second group have little or more banking and payment facilities available around them but many factors drag them back. They have access to banking services but the usage is limited to occasional benefits like for Direct Fund Transfer by the government in welfare schemes or for personal benefit such as the saving or transfer of funds in the case of specific occasions. For example, as a part of the Janadhana Yojana,* the government-sanctioned an overdrawing facility of Rs. 5000 with a low interest and personal accident insurance of Rs. 1 lakh and many more. This attracted many.

The third group is a smaller one due to the government's drive of financial inclusion—a significant number of people who never step into banks and sometimes this is an entirely new word to the people in remote and tribal areas. Here, we need to put in place physical infrastructure like mini-banks and internet and mobile communication systems.

The irony in the current system is that many competitive and useful government-backed schemes in the banking system are targeted at poor villagers and are especially for the betterment of talented young people in rural and semi-urban areas, but no communication and financial service other than distant banks existed to offer these financial opportunities to the targeted people. With our concept of many mini-banks (post office banks) in every village, the third group will decrease further.

During their usage of this initiative, due to low literacy levels, they may fail to understand or may encounter other problems. They will need "instant care" to keep the trust in e-ways intact and also to remove any fear playing on their minds.

Secondly, due to their low exposure to electronic media and other means of awareness regarding the services available to them, they need a "dedicated guide" for counselling and training.

The mini-bank takes all the services the government wishes to provide to every man in the country through a "SOFT (Social, finance and technical) apprentice." This person would be the first point of customer care and act as a dedicated guide to banking and financial-related issues to people like villagers who are new to it all.

They will need to have regular field studies across villages and identity potential candidates that need to be educated about banking and government financial assistance opportunities for the realisation of this dream.

He works in coordination with mini-banks, Village Head and Revenue Development Officer.

Adya laughs.

VVSS: Why you are laughing? What is wrong with my proposal?

---

* Pradhan Mantri Jan-Dhan Yojana (P.M.J.D.Y) is Prime Minister's People Money Scheme is India's National Mission for Financial Inclusion

Adya: There is nothing wrong with your proposal. Villages still have sluggish growth despite each village having many officials including politically-elected representatives such as the Panchayat head and government employees like Village Revenue Officers (VRO) along with Village Assistants in some parts of the country, Village Development Officer (VDO). Yet many villagers do not even know that a modern and technology-enhanced world exists in the country where they live.

Now you are talking about adding another lazy employee. He will also hardly visit the village since no one questions these people.

VVSS: Hold on, these people are not like you think. These people are always energetic.

Adya: Are they deploying Superman to every village?
(laughs)

VVSS: Yes, but please let me finish, Adya.

They are not Superman but much more than that. Guess who they are.

Okay, I will give you a clue; they the most powerful people and are our hope for the country.

Adya: Students.

VVSS: Yes, they are youth who recently graduated from colleges. They are not employed and wish to work on self-development.

Adya: How can they can be deployed across rural areas for this job? How do they benefit?

VVSS: In India, more than 80 percent of students are not financial literate though a few of them hold Doctorates on various subjects. Secondly, government employees who do not have the appropriate theoretical and practical knowledge. What I propose is that every graduate should have to do field-work before applying to government office posts. And even after working with villages and various people they may continue with these efforts with start-up if they wish to. Most significantly, this is a win-win situation for all stakeholders—students—public—government.

Adya: Interesting but how do they receive benefits?

VVSS: For the public, especially the illiterate, counselling and guidance on benefits of banking services and government schemes will be right at their doors.

The government can reach every man in the country and get honest feedback from the field as these students are not permanent employees that will be lazy or alter the feedback.

For the students, their maturity and confidence will soar. During SOFT, they undergo training with various institutes before being sent to rural areas. They will interact with various people and study their cases. For their work, they will be provided a stipend and a certificate which will be an advantage when it comes to getting jobs anywhere in India.

This is more useful for many students who feel they need more skills but often end up in low-level jobs or unemployed due to financial constraints and a lack of the appropriate environment to excel further.

Another important point worth mentioning here: due to great encouragement for the start-ups in India after 2014, several have taken birth in India. Unfortunately, many failed to survive. Yes, I am sure many of these failed due to lack of vision or basic and fundamental qualities. If you are exposed to the industry with field study, the chance of the start-up failing are low.

Hello readers,

Along with Adya, you should also consider how SOFT could be. What would a detailed description on the training, the job characteristics, the job description, stipend amount and eligibility criteria be?

Come forward and brainstorm to enable younger generations build a new India. My ideas are presented in the coming part.

AADHAAR IS A SPLENDID GIFT BUT TRANSACTIONS ARE A CURSE FOR FINANCIAL PRIVACY AND PERSONAL SECURITY

The above heading seems ambiguous, right? But financial privacy, is truly required in everyone's life to maintain one's financial and personal safety.

I narrate a story which I came across in a regional newspaper during my childhood.

In the Southern states of India, Andhra Pradesh Telangana, and in some parts of Tamil Nadu, a majority of parents, including me, have enormous faith in Lord Balaji of Tirupati. We visit this place for our children's success in academics or career or for the fulfillment of any wish.

There was one man in his early forties travelling by train to Tirupati. He lost his bag on the journey. He and his family were not concerned as it did not contain valuables. It held only low denomination new currency bundles drawn from the bank for the journey. They finished their journey and returned home.

One day, his four-year-old little girl disappeared while playing outside late in the evening. Late that night, they received a call from an unknown number asking for a ransom amount of Rs. 14 lakhs. One family member raised an interesting question. Why did the kidnapper demand exactly Rs. 14 lakhs? Why not 10 or 15 or 20? He questioned girl father about his bank balance.

They called from another number and asked if the money was ready or not. On arrangement of the money they would tell them to drop it off. With a gloomy face, the father told kidnapper, "I am not so rich that I can arrange such a huge amount overnight."

"I am giving you till tomorrow afternoon so that you can withdraw the money from your bank account. If you approach the police, your little princess will die."

How did the kidnappers know his bank balance? Were they bank associates or family members who knew the financial status of this man? They wondered whether to approach the police or not. The sun rose and erased the dark, sorrowful night and made every family member rush to explore various options to find a solution.

He eventually decided to draw the money from the bank account and pay the ransom to secure the safe release of his daughter. In a hurry, he was not able to find his passbook. He scolded his wife and she reminded him that before leaving on vacation he had drawn money from the bank. He was the one that should know the whereabouts of the book.

He remembered that the passbook was in the bag lost on the train. He realised that these kidnappers were probably the same people who robbed his bag and came to know his house address, phone number and bank balance. What happened next is irrelevant to us.

Adya: Okay, it is a good story to prove the importance of financial privacy. So far, the Aadhaar is being considered an effective tool in documenting the person's identity and his transaction accountability. However, my question is how do you track and keep the financial transactions without any bias, redundancy and exclusion? Do you have a solution?
(smiled)

VVSS: Yes, I do.

First, tell me why banks and other private entities need access to Aadhaar data?

To me, putting aside the few benefits including quick verification of identity, it is not justified and I strongly feel it leaves a threat like a knife at your neck. A simple example I can state with confidence that nobody knows my 15-year-old bank account number but many know an Aadhaar number that is a couple years old and my date of birth can be extracted from the Aadhaar card.

One day, a national bank representative came to my house in my village with his bank-issued machine, which is called a micro-ATM. I did not know what it was. He asked me to put my thumb on the machine fingerprint scanner. I did it with a smile without any questions as I was still clueless about what the machine was. After a few seconds, he could tell me all my bank account numbers and their balance status.

He was my student when he was in primary school. I asked how he was able to retrieve my balances from all my bank accounts. He told me that he had taken my Aadhaar number collected from my illiterate mother and upon authentication with my thumb, all Aadhaar-linked account information popped up automatically.

Do you feel this incident is safe for me and my financial privacy? Of course, this particular incident may not be harmful as he was my student and lived opposite my home.

I think the government taking a wrong step by allowing Aadhaar metadata access to all third-party players.

The solution is very simple,

Do not encourage Aadhaar number-based transactions. Instead, link all accounts to Aadhaar and carry out transactions with the old practice of account number or mobile number (as proxy account number) or virtual address. The last two methods leave the customer with the chance to change these whenever he wishes. Finally, if cruel people gain these three numbers they cannot extract any personal and financial data, however, with Aadhaar he can.

Secondly and more importantly, do not allow any private entities like Paytm to access the Aadhaar database for the verification of identity and other parameters. Let these entities maintain the previous method of verification or let them put the request to verify with the Aadhaar department but direct access to Aadhaar data is not at all desirable.

Adya: You are completely discouraging the usage of the Aadhaar. Then how can you claim it is a splendid gift?

VVSS: See! In the month of July in 2014, I went to Delhi on duty for three months. On the very first day, I was welcomed with a shock in the Delhi Transport department where I was pickpocketed. It left me on the road without a single paisa and at the police station for hours. With the help of my friend I finally reached the camp.

During my stay in the Delhi, on weekends, I used to visit one of my college friends who worked in a reputed American-based IT company as a Team Lead and earned Rs. 2 lakhs a month. One day, someone knocked on the door while my friend was in the bathroom. Through the peephole of the door, I saw a person with a government-subsidised LPG cylinder on his shoulder. I called to my friend, "Gas cylinder has arrived." He asked me to take the cylinder and pay the man Rs. 1200.

After his shower, I asked why the gas was so much costlier in his city. I assumed the price of the gas is the same across the country. Then he smiled and asked me to give him the bill. I apologised and told him I had forgotten to demand the bill. His smile turned into a small laugh. It was a black-market cylinder. I was shocked that people were paying 4 times the original cost being offered by the government.

Despite many years of staying in Delhi, my friend never took any LPG connection due to time constraints and the huge administration work involved. He was comfortable getting the cylinder with just a phone call and Rs. 1200. In 2016, I called him on the phone to wish him for his marriage and asked if he was still getting LPG from the black-market vendor. His reply was surprising. Due to the DBTL (Direct Benefit Transfer for LPG) scheme, the supply to black market had dropped. Since DBTL mandates every consumer link their Aadhaar number and accounts for the direct transfer of the subsidy. Bogus connections were eliminated leaving the black-market empty-handed. So, he finally took a gas connection from the gas agency which cost him two-days leave from the office, he usually used this leave to visit his native place.

Here it is evident that Aadhaar addressed the problem of multiple identity/proxy consumers by which the black-market gained dominance. Now only genuine people get the government-subsidised LPG cylinders. As per the news reports, this Aadhaar linkage scheme alone weeded out more than 3 crore bogus connections leaving the government to profit. It was the same the case with the public distribution system (PDS) where bogus beneficiary cards have been reduced greatly to pave the way for genuine consumers to get the goods at a cheaper price. Such success stories linked with the Aadhaar are significant in number.

The concept of the Aadhaar reduced the malpractice and corruption in the system and it is undoubtedly a unique and truly magnificent gift to India. There is abundant potential to ease the administration in the country. I would like to tell you an old saying my grandmother said.

"Over-usage of anything often yields counter production which costs you much more than what you benefited from it so far."

This is exactly the case with the Aadhaar invading financial and personal privacy due to over-usage by the financial institutes.

If everyone was truly honest then there would not have been any malpractice in this country. Indeed, the concept of the Aadhaar would not find any space in this world. Such social structure is highly hypothetical and sometimes called superstition.

There must be some sort of mechanism to address evil problem of multiple identities. Here, everybody admits that only Aadhaar address this issue. Every citizen is renamed with a permanent and unique digital number forever. This number only dies by appearing on a death certificate.

Now everyone is able to mention their digital name everywhere and the identity cannot be played with. This also very useful in health administration as everyone mentions the same number whenever they undergo treatment at various places and their information can be accessed in case of emergencies if all the medical institutes are integrated. This alone can streamline the entire banking system.

Since Aadhaar number is being shared everywhere in daily life as identity and address proof such as obtaining a mobile SIM card from a gully shop, in educational institutes and other private entities. So, your Aadhaar number is being freely shared. Now only authentication is required to access the data which is very easy with the illiterate.

Hello,

Let's move to another part, where you can use your IQ to crush my ideas with your own brainstorming.

A detailed description on the SOFT apprentice like training, job characteristics, job description, stipend fixation, eligibility criteria and more—come design and enable our younger generations to build a new India.

TEAM WORK REQUIRED OR NOT

Implementation of ideas like demonetisation and a cashless economy without any major hurdles and security breaches across the country are only possible if all concerned departments are playing as a team with exemplary coordination and synchronisation.

At the time of demonetisation, India's largest transport provider, the railways were completely unaligned with the financial departments. The whole railway department was not prepared to realise "payments can be made without hard cash in this world." It caused the lot of struggles for the public and became an undermining force for the drive by becoming a place of paradise for miscreants who wished to change the old currency illegally.

A meticulous movement should be made in a coordinated manner by all affected stakeholders as a team.

Adya: Yeah! In my introductory classes for my business management course, many professors repeatedly emphasise that teamwork is important for the success of any organization or even family life. No matter how the team is formed everyone should work relentlessly towards a common goal.

VVSS: Then guess! Who are so important in this mission for a cashless in India?

Adya: Usually, one pays one's earnings for their day-to-day needs like rations, milk, clothes, petrol, medicine etc to both government and private corporations like electricity, telephone, hospital and various taxes. To enable these payments and bills to be made without hard cash, a few of the government entities should work in synchronisation. Right?

VVSS: Why are only these affected? Can you be more elaborate?

Adya: These departments have regular business with the public, esecially with the lower section of people in India.

Take the case of the banking system.

I have a credit card, debit card, IMPS access, internet banking and e-wallet, but I am not able to pay to my milkman.

He says the bank is located around 10 km from his home.

It takes 3 to 4 hours to complete transactions if you line up there.

It is evident that a cashless economy is going to be a dream if the best of the banking system is not within reach of the common-man.

In my opinion, the current banking system is one of the main paths of corruption activities. So the banking system should sanctify all its business by establishing customer identity integrity and the development of its infrastructure for it to be in everyone's reach.

VVSS: Hold on. What is customer identity integrity?

Adya: Currently, multiple accounts exist with various proxy names but in reality only one person is the customer. If the data integrity is accomplished then this situation cannot take place.

Next, banks should work towards building the nation along with the goal of banking development. The Reserve Bank of India (RBI) completely failed in my eyes as it should have established a unique payment system across India before demonetisation. Perhaps, then demonetisation would not be required. Just look at this screenshot from bookmyshow.com I did while making a payment for the movie Dangal. You can clearly see what I mean.

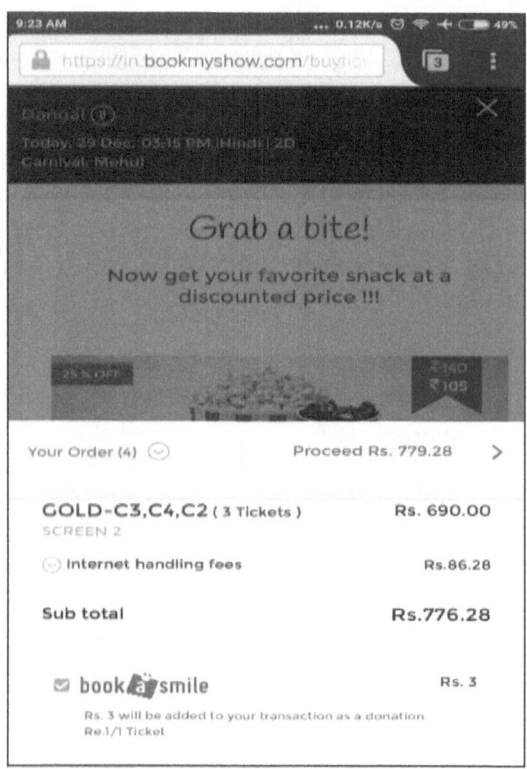

Above projected screen-shot is taken from bookmyshow.com while booking movie ticket.

Here my effort is to highlight one of the most discouraging factor for online transactions as a part of cashless society that.

"around 11.2% is charged as internet handling charges if one goes for booking on line with any of my digital payment means."

Therefore,

Whenever I am looking forward for watching any show with my family consist of 5 to 7 member...

I have to shell out around 150 to 200 rupees as internet handling charges.

Why should anybody pay?

Aadhaar Facility Centers: Nowadays, government and private entities are asking for our Aadhaar number with updated details at every step in our daily lives.

Unfortunately in some areas, for nearly 30 villages only one Aadhaar enrollment centres are available and levy heavy charges. How can daily-wage workers reach these centres and even enroll or make queries. We cannot expect these people to embrace online solutions as they mostly technically illiterate.

Since Aadhaar is meant to be the centre of all activities of administration and finance matters, it requires facilities everywhere to ensure every citizen can create and modify their Aadhaar cards. Otherwise, the common man is going to be badly affected.

Ministry of Finance: Mother of all departments in the financial context.

Transparency can be increased with information technology and cashless transaction. Take the case of public ration depots where the government distributes rice, kerosene etc at subsidised prices. Here the big question is, are all the goods distributed to targeted people or diverted to the black market? Had this been made transparent with the use of the technology and Aadhaar framework, the finance department would gain a lot of profit.

Though the efforts of this department towards digitalisation is significant it still falls behind in capitalising on the opportunity that emerged with Aadhaar and demonetisation.

The Ministry of Commerce and Industry should have kept in mind, the Aadhaar is launched with the aim of curbing proxy identities so that duplicate and illegal transactions are evaded. This ministry should have worked towards the mission since launch of the AADHAAR. Now many have the various businesses using various family members or their own proxy identity to avoid taxes and other legal obligations.

VVSS: Except taxes what are the other legal obligations to fulfill?

Adya: Yes, you are right. If the business is truly micro in nature, there is perhaps only the obligation of tax applicable. Having numerous micro businesses, if connected officially, translates to a large business and one needs to fulfill the various legal obligations such as auditing, employee welfare schemes, etc.

But due to continuous running of these businesses as a cluster of micro businesses on various fake names, it is not possible for the government to track down these companies. Furthermore, there is no mandatory clause for a license that these business should transact in e-payments.

Ministry of IT: Perhaps as per as my opinion concerned till recent years this was the most underperforming department in India. This is evident with the status of BSNL (Bharath Sanchar Nigam Limited) in the Indian people's mind.

Take the case of AT&T (American Telephone & Telegraph) which is the world's largest telecommunications company. Our BSNL is unable to serve our people effectively despite having 125 Cr people and the government backing it.

My intention is very clear that communication is very important in our life and for the betterment of the country. Even it is required to enhance the e-transaction base across the country.

Ministry of HRD: I have to recollect and highlight a great quote from the legendary former president of America, Abraham Lincoln on the education of children and their impact on the adult.

> *"Teach the children,*
> *So it will not be*
> *Necessary*
> *To teach the adults..."*

This explains all my thoughts here. This ministry enjoys the fresh and energetic blood of 356 million young people to do any kind of miracle in India. Student power is beyond the comprehension of anyone.

I strongly believe that relevant education and training are pre-requisites for anyone to behave in a specific manner. Unfortunately, the Indian education system so far always tried copy-cat methods. I am not fully against this but it should have been crafted to align with nationally inherent values and ethics.

One fundamental themes, I would like to mention here is financial literacy like taxation and its importance in the country development, Indian values and nutrition science are not imparted beyond 10th standard (very few streams cover this) in our schooling system. I think the syllabus should be crafted in ways which impart and emphasise fundamentals and tools for life in society and should continue till the graduation level along-with the main subjects one chooses. One thing worth mention here is that, in primary schools we teach children currency identification and handling. But is it possible now? With all the current multiple payment systems we have today.

VVSS: Adya, you have shown the need for basic values and fundamentals to be included in education so that everyone in all areas of life we interact with will follow the same ideas and rules. Readers, do you have any ideas? You all have the experience of various stages of academic and professional life.

Adya: Okay, I have a lot of ideas that emerged when I faced many problems with my employees' behaviour in my company. Sometimes I wondered;

How did they get through their academics without knowing the fundamentals?

How did these people lead life when they stepped out of the company? We can attribute this to a lot of inadequacies in our education system.

Let me move on to another department which has a big role in the Indian economy and development and therefore in the creation of a cashless society. It is none other than the Ministry of Railways.

In this technologically-advanced era the railways failed to match their e-facilities with conventionally available facilities outside. Indeed, it did not show the technical maturity shown by small travel agencies. Booking a seat in travel companies with all the payment systems is so easy.

Railways discourage electronic ways as travellers who do not find alternative means have to follow the troublesome methods of the railways' online booking system. They charge much more from a person if he books the ticket online for the same journey. This is very high if one stretches his journey with multiple breaks due to the unavailability of a single train. He has to generate each ticket with all the extra charges for all trains he boards during his journey. The railways should find ways to ensure the TTE-*Gundagiri* reduced to zero and enforce them only to do their core duty with kindness, the way other private players of public transport do.

However, except for a few areas, the railway has changed fast in recent years which will hopefully align itself with the mission of a new India. Let me move on to the next department, which is full of patriotism, intelligence, hardship and a disciplined workforce.

Can you guess which one?

VVSS: Defense.

Adya: Yes, you are right. This department enjoys a unique quality of nearly 100 percent literate people under its wings. I think, as per the current scenario, these disciplined forces are under-utilized for the social and economic development of India. They are indeed idle citizens so any reforms should start from the defense premises.

Unfortunately, this ministry is also not aligned with social and technical changes. These organisations are still running old practices despite having the executive powers to implement them within their boundaries. For example, the Canteen Service Department still levies a transaction fees on purchase of goods and pays through POS whereas in a private small shop there are no charges.

Of course, this is not the scene across India. Very few canteen stores are charging any extra amount on bills. Finally, despite the uniform and disciplined services, they are also not in line with cashless operations. This is a very important department that could be used for the betterment of society.

The Ministry of Law: In my eyes it is to protect the interests of the people in the country from people with corrupt interests. However, laws are made only when people commit crimes repeatedly and not before this. If they proactively anticipated these and even continuously changed the legal framework to match technological advancements then a cashless economy with zero corruption would prevail.

VVSS: Yes, you are right. But as per as my opinion, these things change as the time passes and as per each government. I have the strong apprehension that even if you are not doing the right thing at the right time, the right thing is automatically judged as the wrong thing.

Because of this, a single person or a single reform cannot do any expected miracles and we absolutely need teamwork in the country to progress.

Hello friends,

Adya pointed out a lot discouraging factors across India that impede people from turning cashless. I liked her proposal for a disciplined Defence department and mature students must be the forerunners in implementing reforms in India. Right?

I think, with instances from your daily life, you as a citizen of this country might have produced similar thoughts in response to an embarrassing situation faced or witnessed in various sections of your life. Take a piece of the paper, summarise it and share it with us. It will become part of the next edition published.

I came across the 2016–17 economic survey covering team recommendations like JAM (Janadhan-AADHAAR-Mobile), UBI-Universal Basic Income, etc to root out black money and thus corruption in India. Let's move forward to discuss these aspects, let's see whether these ideas are feasible with the current multiple payment platforms and other administrative blockades.

Are you ready?

No, drink a cup of water.

Flip the page.

PART – III

Pillars For New India

"Eradication of corruption and inequalities.
So far these remain the buzzwords of all election campaigns with every political and ruling party in India since independence.
Have they ever been achieved or at least remembered till the time arrived for the next election?"

Since independence, every government has promised Indian citizens their life would be secured by rooting out corruption. Unfortunately, this statement is still valid. Many political parties have mastered putting the same wine in a new bottle to lure voters.

Change in corruption's style is forced due to technological evolution not any government efforts. Even if they claimed to do any work toward the eradication of corruption, that is only passive in nature.

Everybody should also acknowledge that the main cause of corruption is people earning money overnight in unlawful ways. The question arises that banks and payment systems, despite being in existence for centuries have not changed the situation significantly. This is mainly due to the fact that none of the banks ever see themselves as builders of a clean society. They only do the accounting at the end of the day by looking at the balance sheet like a corporate business.

In developed countries, they succeeded in these aspects by putting good banking and efficient payment systems in place. Until now, India never wholeheartedly attempted to bring about a system change and did only patchwork in response to incidents.

After the Indian planning commission was re-engineered into the NITI Ayog by the current government the push for a digital economy is like never before. In this perspective, a few interesting things are featured in the economic survey 2016–2017. It suggested many ideas, may be borrowed or created like the JAM (Janadhan-AADHAAR-Mobile) and UBI (universal basic income) concepts with the intention to kill the evil of corruption.

UBI mandates the government to give a minimum basic income to the all of its citizens unconditionally. This concept is not new as a few countries are already using this scheme. My concern is that in a highly populated and extremely diverse country like India, this scheme is going to lose before the contest starts.

Take the case of the MGNREGA (Mahatma Gandhi National Rural Employment Guarantee) that mandates the government to provide a minimum of a 100 days of work to all citizens. This is launched exclusively with this simple statement. No conditions regarding its implementation have been formulated, if formulated they are weaker and allow people to exploit them. It certainly raised the corruption level and burdened the Indian economy and had a negligible contribution to the GDP. The list of negatives is exhaustive and will be covered in later pages.

As per as my opinion, despite the indispensable contribution towards nation building, these five groups of people have been treated with little respect in India. At least now they must receive their due respect and continuous care by implementing the UBI to avoid any further damage to society and in turn to the country.

I think, by this time, you might have drawn your own list of those five groups or are trying to contradict my view. If your list ready?

Adya: Yes, I am wondering who they are and already trying to prepare my list of their importance but tell me a little about the economic survey.

VVSS: The economic survey is the report card of Indian economic development for the past 12 months. It highlights the changes that have taken place in the economy, the progress of various development programs and any other policy implementation introduced by the government during the previous year. The finance ministry carries out this survey and presents it in both houses of the Indian Parliament before the budget session. I think this is enough for you to understand.

Now tell me your list of the five people who are crucial to India and its future prospects.

Adya: Tell me yours and I will compare mine with it and then reveal it.

VVSS: My list is very simple. And this model of the UBI is going to be effective and easily implementable with my payment system of 'one India, one currency and one payment system,' which is IPay.

I would like to introduce the first person on my nation builders list.

IF 'SHE' IS IGNORED, THE WORLD ENDS

One evening, I was out jogging with my friends. We passed a construction site on the outskirts of our city. We heard the crying of a small baby. We stopped and searched the site. We were shocked to find the crying baby. Right under the evening sun, the baby was in a temporary swing-bed made with a towel hung between two sticks. As we were wondering who left this baby here, a woman rushed towards us. We decided to interrogate her about the ill-treatment of the baby.

She grabbed the baby and we asked who she was and why the baby was left there unattended under the sun.

She said, "Saab! Only a couple of hours passed since I left this baby to sleep."

We asked her to take the baby to a cool place. She took it inside to feed it. After some time, she returned and we told her that the baby had been crying continuously for the past five minutes. We asked why she had not come instantly.

We were very shocked by her reply.

She said, "I was taking the bricks to the next floor from the first floor in a human transportation chain. If I left my position for a moment to go to my baby, then the chain gets broken and the contractor will scold or threaten me with wage reduction. Sometimes, he even threatens that he will not allow me to work the next day if I take frequent breaks during work."

We don't have any words nor any resources to rescue her and her baby from the site. This incident made us think deeply and even stopped our jogging session, we left and sat under a big banyan tree to discuss this. We cursed her husband, contractor and fellow workers for not letting the mother take care of her infant.

One of my friends wondered why we were scolding the contractor. He helped the mother by giving her work. Had he refused her work on the basis of breaks for the baby she would have lost her wage and become reliant on her husband's wages. Of course, if he was fond of alcohol then she and the baby would have stayed hungry.

A few of us supported his argument and shared experiences like 'I was never left alone for even one minute by my mother.' But we realised we were born privileged and not all of us could be. Another friend asked what sin that mother and baby had committed sin that they were deprived of basics. What a contrast.

Another friend, who is well-educated and usually quiet and calm, raised his voice for the first time, "Can we arrange for any constant income to these mothers in our village so that our next generation is secure and has well-groomed young people who do not experience starvation ever?"

Everybody stared at him and replied that we all walk the roads every day and eat food we got through our parents earnings. How can we arrange such a scheme?

He replied, of course, we cannot but we can collect the funds and give the necessary food to the mother and baby.

Such stories have been around and everywhere for centuries, unfortunately. Just imagine the world without motherhood.

I would like to share another story with you about a mother in my village who lost her teaching job after becoming pregnant.

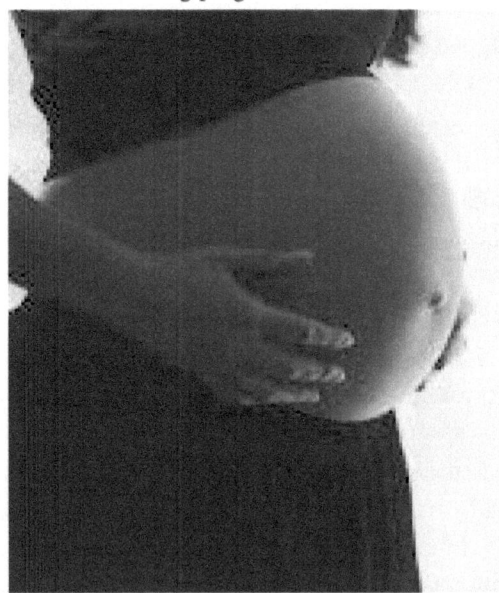

This was my relative, Devi's story. There is a small private school located around one-and-a-half kilometres from her home. She used to walk to work and earned Rs. 1000 per month. After becoming pregnant, she had to stop walking and lost the job as she is not a government employee does not work for a corporate where maternity leave with full salary is granted. Her husband, who is fond of booze, brings home hardly Rs. 100 per day after a visit to the booze shop. She is never shocked or upset even when he comes home with no money in his pocket and sometimes she is happy and says, "Thanks to God, my husband returned home alive or unhurt after heavy drinking."

After giving birth to a baby boy, she again thanked God for not bestowing her with a baby girl, otherwise her family would even expel her from the family. After she recovered from the delivery, she found a job in a milk dairy shop where she needs to work one hour in the morning and evening. She gets Rs. 600 and half a litre of milk daily as salary. So her baby at least gets its nutrition with milk. She cannot do full-fledged work until the baby starts schooling. Sadly, she became pregnant again as her husband never understood the problem of having two kids with a low income.

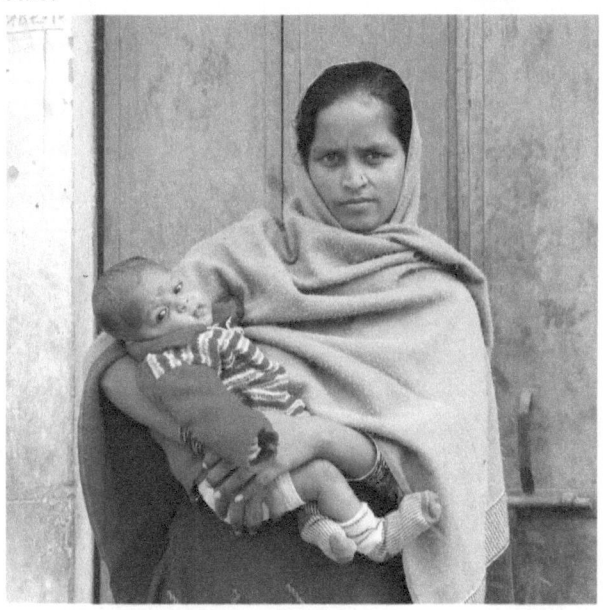

I think you might have realised the burdens and pain of women once they become pregnant. Till a few months ago, she earned equally with her husband. Now, she has become a poor earner to become a good mother. Consequently, the income of the household is reduced to half and the expenses have climbed exponentially due to an increased need for food and medicine for the well-being of both mother and child. This story may not make any difference or any impact on a rich couple but it is a huge setback to the poor.

Leave the struggles of these people and think of the kids who are going to be the pillars of the next generation alongside the children of the rich. Can't we take care of them to the extent that they are at least decently nourished and well-educated enough to take care of their motherland in the times to come?

It is very difficult for a family to have a healthy life on one wage in India. Sometimes, people are forced to leave their children by the garbage or in bus stops, do illegal work or sell their babies with a heavy heart to human traffickers for a meagre amount. After centuries of a civilized society, we are still not able to secure women and their interests.

If she and the baby received a Universal Basic Income for women from the day she takes on the responsibility of motherhood to the time her children grow up, they will never be victim of financial loss and threats from family, society and their husbands. With consistent income she can groom herself and her kids without any kind of insecurity, which provides a solid foundation for the next generation with well-nourished young children.

Adya: Some may be in understanding that This will encourage these people to keep having children so they can continuously receive this income. The same is being abused in countries like England in the same manner. This idea is not logical and will affect the county's economy.

VVSS: Of course, this seems to be valid. But with well customized scheme of UBIM in the proposed JAMI frame work, your claim never be outcome in anyway.

After this, I am sure that there will be a sharp reduction of orphans, beggars, the flesh trade, human-trafficking and other illegal trades. The implementation of this scheme is quite easy with the IPay system

Hello, my beloved readers,

Adya and I figured out the best possible way for the implementation of UBI for women. However, I request you, your friends and family members to use your brilliance to support these ideas and point out problems if any are found we will meet on this topic on in next part.

IF HIS SWEAT STOPS, THE WORLD STARVES

"One day, a speeding car came to a halt on a narrow road. The driver, who was driving with a yummy burger in one hand, had noticed an aged man crossing the road without looking at the traffic."

The rich driver got out and started scolding the old man with very harsh words and further quoted "Your life is not even of equal value to the burger in my hand."

The old man stopped him, "Saabji! I would like to tell you one thing. That burger took birth in my hand and left my home to be delicious in your mouth."

No matter how much currency you have it will never fill your belly. Only food, irrespective of your financial status, will help you survive. Consequently, food-yielding farmers are nothing but another form of God. Over the time, due to the rise of economic competition between companies and countries, this God is reduced to the ground to the status of the low and untouchable.

During my childhood, my parents used to send me to the agricultural fields with a small bag in hand. Since we do not have any land nor even a small hut, we had a rented house. We begged the farmer to gift us a little grains or pulses or ground nuts. Our bags used to overflow with everything. But nowadays, in same village with the same hardworking people there, no one gifts even the shell of a nut to anyone.

Now you might blame the farmers for becoming miserliness or greedy over time. But keep in mind, this is not reality. Most farmers have sold their land to big landlords and become workers under them. Earlier, they were the boss now they have been reduced to the farmhand. How can they gift anything to anyone without the permission of their arrogant landlord?

This situation came about due to the reduction in farming, especially among kind and pure-hearted farmers. Now, they are slaves to evil *Benami* farmers who are corporate minded. These farmers have mastered how to avail the government schemes by using these poor farmers and they sustain their profits.

I met a friend from a tribal area during my training and he narrated his story;

He comes from a small tribal village where a few hundred people live. This village is beautiful and surrounded by hills and forests, except for one side which opens to the rest of the world. Here, a gravel road leads to another village with a big bridge made of the stones between them.

This village does not have a single shop with all the basics. One day, a person from the same village decided to open a shop with a little capital so that all the villagers need not to rush to the next village for their daily needs.

This small-time businessman started planning but he finally opened the shop on the other side of the bridge and not in the village.

The villagers questioned him, "Why have you opened the shop far away from the village? There is not much difference for our villagers in distance."

His reply shocked everyone. If he opened the shop in the village, he would lose business frequently in the rainy season due to this bridge, which usually sank during the rain due to a heavy downpour from the hilltops.

It disconnects the village from the rest of the world. After considering this fact, he gave up the idea of the shop in that village and set it up on the other side of the bridge. Now he would get business from both villages when there was no rain and one village when there was rain.

This is the perfect SWOT (strength, weakness, opportunity and threats) analysis at a lower level. See the analysis he made before setting up a small grocery shop? He gave profit more weightage and less important to the fellow inhabitants of his village.

Unfortunately, a farmer never thinks of this analysis. He has only a blind belief in his farming despite all of the business factors are uncertain. If he did, perhaps we would one tell our children that centuries ago, there used to be farmers.

On 12 Oct 2014, every farmer rejoiced with the hope of a good farm yield due to good rainfall for two days. This happiness was short lived and turned to disaster with a HUDHUD STORM that destroyed the crops with powerful wind blowing at the speed of 185 km/h (155 mph).

All of a sudden their hundreds of hours of sweat and thousands of rupees were wasted. Every farmer would have thought of the uncertainties but only a few could endure. The remaining struggled and a few even went on to commit suicide.

The government provided a little relief with loan waviers and other monetary aid. This little relief comes only in response to big disasters and lot of suicides thereafter.

In the present unpredictable climate due to global warming, farming is almost like dancing on the sword's edge. All the basic requirements for farming is absolutely uncertain.

Take the case of the main requirement for farming, "water." 80 to 90 percent of farmers are still uncertain about the availability of water and if rains or not, will it be enough?

A farmer is the only businessman in the world that starts business without having surety of return on capital. He also knows if one cycle yields zero, he has hardly anything left to eat the next year and the pressure of both bank and private money lenders is added. It is not a shock he finds a solution in suicide.

If unfortunately, a farmer never thinks of SWOT analysis. He has only a blind belief in his farming despite the business factors being uncertain. If he did, perhaps we would one day tell our children that centuries ago, there used to be farmers.

Nevertheless, he still continues to do this business. If he stops, the world stops.

Adya: What could be the best solution for the Gods that feed us?

VVSS: The best solution is that farming should be done in partnership with the government across India.

Adya: What is wrong with you? How can you ask the government to manage the farming across the large country of India?

VVSS:	No large area! Thanks to industrialism and greedy politicians, much of our farm land has been converted for industries or for residential area or they are now millions of vacant plots. India is looking to other small countries for importing pulses and other goods to meet its own short supply.
Adya:	Still it is a huge area to farm for one entity.
VVSS:	The government will not do the farming. It will only provide the investment to all the farmers by purchasing the raw material, so that farmers can sweat more confidently in the fields. For this they must be given substantial capital in proportion to the quantity of land.

Universal basic investment—I have borrowed the premise of the idea from the concept of UBI (universal Basic Income).

Under the Universal Basic investment scheme, the government provide automatic credit in proportion to the land he owns to enable a farmer to purchase all the necessary raw material like pesticides and seeds. When the yield is sold by the farmer, he will deposit the amount with nominal interest with the government. Or in case, his yield is swept away by any natural disasters, this credit will be automatically waived.

> **Loan waiver: Maharashtra govt receives 10 lakh applications**
>
> BHAVIKA JAIN, TNN • CITY
> 9 HOURS AGO
>
> MUMBAI: The state government has so far received nearly 10 lakh applications from farmers to be a part of loan-waiver scheme.
>
> The state government has started accepting online applications since July 24 and has also set up 26000 centres to assist the farmers to fill the forms.

Since the start of the second half of 2017, India has faced a series of the floods and other natural calamities causing millions of acres of agricultural crops to wash away.

You may rise the point that both the Union and State governments have announced and disbursed thousands of the crores for the loss they incurred.

Yes, you are right. But do you feel that every small farmer has got the benefit from this hectic process and do you think it will sufficiently compensate the cost of the raw material? I am not calculating here the sweat the farmer invested; in our country the sweat has no value.

Under my solution, farming is in a Government-Farmer Partnership (GFP) through Universal Basic Investment.

Adya: But it may raise questions from metropolitan personalities. Why should the government invest in every grain harvested in India? They always perceive farming as a business and never see them as belly-feeders.

VVSS: One thing needs to be remembered; if a person wants to live on this planet he needs three basic things;

Pure air
Clean water
Sufficient food

The first two are provided by nature or needs some sort of processing method in some places to provide. However, the third needs human efforts to yield from this environment. So obviously, one of the prime responsibilities of the government is to secure food for its citizens.

And not by importing from other countries. A country must be self-reliant in terms of at least food. All other businesses are secondary.

I hope my scheme will give the necessary boost up to every farmer in the county so I request my readers to craft ideas too. *"Save ourselves by saving our nutrients."*

YOUNG BLOOD IS SMARTER AND WILL HELP THE WORLD PROSPER

> Young people - with their dynamism, their energy and their inherent understanding of our interconnected world - have much to teach us. Increased educational attainment, advances in technology and the spread of information have made this generation the best educated, most connected and most informed in history
>
> — *Kofi Annan*

One day at a small bus stand in my city, I noticed a small group of young people walking across all the bus terminals looking for their bus. They desperately failed to identity the bus which would take them to their village.

One of the group asked me the time of arrival of their red and blue coloured bus.

I did not understand initially why they referred to it by colour instead of by destination. I asked, "Where do you want to go?"

"We have to go to Mutcherla village and every day at this time, a red and blue bus usually comes to this terminal. Today, we are not able to find the bus though we looked for an hour."

I noticed a bus standing at the bus terminal with a display board that read 'Mutcherla.' I told them the green bus goes to this village.

They said, "Sir, our bus is red and blue."

"That new bus might have been given our route."

They boarded the bus with me.

I took the seat in the bus next to Krishna and relaxed.

I asked, "Your dressing and appearance is smart but you don't know how to read."

"We have been hotel workers since childhood. Due to my poor parents' condition, they always want us to help them by at-least taking food from my house to the farmland where they work for a daily wage. Later, I was given the responsibility of the sheep for day-care. Every day I had to take them to vacant farm land for grazing. Though I had an enormous interest in doing primary school, it never happened."

What could he have become if his parents had not given him these responsibilities and sent him to school. Of-course, we cannot blame his parents.

One evening when I was out for a walk in my village, I noticed the same boy I met at the bus stand. I asked my friend, "Why is he in our village?"

The response was shocking. This boy was thrown out of the hotel because he attempted to rob the cashier. This usually happens when kids are not fundamentally right and are exposed to higher living style. In an effort to live this life, they follow short and easy paths like robbery.

In my opinion, education with proper values is must. However, after gaining a fair education qualification, they leave college/school without any employment. Over a period of leisure, they usually find a quick solution with the belief that it will pave the way forward out of their current problems. But these quick-fix solutions like robbery or chain-snatching, cyber-crime etc soon become costlier.

Adya: Do you feel that everyone who leaves college without employment are defaulters?

VVSS: You cannot put all your eggs in one basket since each egg needs a different temperature, duration and other environmental conditions to hatch and turn into chicks.

In town, there are a lot of small employment opportunities starting from sweeper to shopkeeper but in rural areas, what are the employment opportunities except seasonal farming?

Students, who study with the help of struggling parents and government aid, after their completion of schooling or college, have to learn more skills to get a job anywhere.

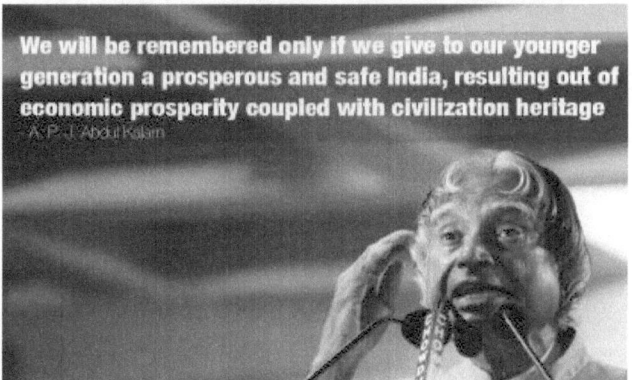

But here is the big question, are they able to afford their basic requirements? I have seen many young people working part-time for a small income to get basic food and shelter.

Who is to be blamed for their failure and responsible for their future?

- Their parents
- Teachers and Schools/colleges
- Social structure
- Government

Parents cannot be blamed as they have already made a lot of sacrifices and groomed their children with their sweat and blood.

Poor schools do not see the quality of teachers, technology and other programmes built to shape young people for careers.

The two elements of social structure and government have an immense responsibility to ensure that the younger generation must groomed to become responsible citizens. In my opinion, the government has failed.

We have the largest illiterate population in the world and there is a wide gap between social and economic sections of society in education too.

Soon after leaving college, the middle class and rich have no problems as they already the skill and good financial and social support. But the poor must be aided financially and socially so they can at least fulfill their basic needs.

If they are well-groomed and supported, they will always feel indebted to this society and country. However, we have to design methods of implementation so that this goes unchallenged forever and it should also take care of the burden on union budget expenses. Share your opinion and your proposal will find a place in the next book.

> The young generation of today is globally connected. They want to live in an equitable and efficient India. We have to be ready for this, and work for this.
>
> — *Narendra Modi*

Humanity Should Live Longer; Later or Early You Are in Need

> *"To deny people their human rights is to challenge their very humanity."*
>
> *– Nelson Mandela*

I frequently notice people on the road, begging for money in the hot sun. When I was young, I asked my father why these people beg instead of doing work.

He said, "They cannot do any work since they are handicapped or senior citizens who have been discarded by their family."

As I was fully fit and getting everything, I needed at the time, I said, "If one leg is paralyzed then they can do work with their hands and vice-versa. So why are they not working instead of sitting on the road?"

My father smiled and said, "No private employer willingly employs a handicapped person. The poor are abundant in number in India. If a man employs a healthy yet poor at the same salary then he can get more work done from him.

Take the case of our tea shop, where one boy works round the clock. He serves the tea at the shop and to nearby places in the morning and evening. The rest of the time, he works at the owner's house. For all this work, he is paid Rs. 500 and given the leftover food from the owner's kitchen."

Even in the government, there is a very small number of positions reserved for handicapped people. As of today, 3% is reserved. They have to prove their handicap and be assessed by a doctor. If they are even one percent short of the level of disability required, they are not eligible. Though the reservation is there, these posts are rarely filled.

Education is also not possible for them as in the case of healthy people. Due to physical and mental impairments, they cannot compete.

Adya: Wait, I disagree with the last statement about the competence of the handicapped. One physically handicapped person topped the prestigious UPSC (Union Public Service Commission) in 2014. Her name is Ms. Ira Singhal.

VVSS: I read about her on multiple occasions. She suffers from scoliosis. I would like to remind you that her journey to becoming an IAS officer was not easy. Despite having unmatched talent and dedication, she had to fight a legal battle for four years.

Did you know?

She received a lot of support from her beloved and able parents at every stage since childhood and through the legal battle. It is an inspiring story. But this is not the case with other people who come from humbler backgrounds with unsupportive parents.

The disabled are now given a pension in a few parts of the country but that is on a selection basis. The government have lot of stuff on the drawing boards for this community but their life has not changed due to poor implementation combined with bias born out of religion, caste and race.

Therefore, the time has come to implement unconditional Universal basic income for the handicapped (UBIH). They must be provided with consistent income so they need not to waste an entire day hunting for their food. If they are provided basic income, I am sure they will also become productive citizens. There will be a drastic reduction in begging and child trafficking.

YOU ARE SOON BECOME OLDER

"Respect your elders, learn from the people who have walked the way before you, respect them.
Someday sooner than you could even imagine you are going to be old too."

—Unknown

Whenever I go to the terrace of my house in my village, I am shocked to see an old woman older than seventy carrying dry grass on her heads for the owner of the paddy field to his cow shed. Thereafter she clears away all the cow and bull dung and carries it to another piece of the owner's farmland. She performs this work twice a day, in the morning and evening. She also cooks food in her son's house which is located diagonally to my house. Whenever she seeks rest, they curse her and her daughter-in-law even beats her on the head with the kitchen vessels. Meanwhile, her daughter-in-law is always glued to the television, watching serials. Her meek son never ever dares to speak up for his mother.

One day, I asked him, "Why are you not supporting your old mother? She gave birth and struggled her entire life to bring you up for more than forty years. In return, you are not able to feed her proper food and not able to ensure she is respected at your house."

His response was shocking. "My wife threatens to leave the house forever if I interfere and speaks in my mother's favour."

This is the case, whether the family is rich or poor. We frequently read that old parents are discarded by their children.

They gave all their effort and energy for the betterment of the next generation. In return, we give them disrespect, social isolation and insecurity. Consequently, old beggars and suicides among old people are on the rise.

Every contractor and other physical work-related employer looks for young people and pay them very little. Their bad work environment causes age-related health ailments to arise sooner. Gradually, they become weaker, cannot get wage employment and have to depend on their family or go hungry.

We have to admit the fact that our veterans or the builders of the current nation are grossly-neglected and deprived of their basic needs. We should at least wake up now and protect their dignity.

Retired employees from the government and private organisations get wholesome pensions along with other benefits like free medical facilities. They still feel insecure due to a reduced income. So, what about these retired people from a poor background whose income suddenly becomes zero?

The government has the responsibility to ensure a healthier and more respectful life for these people. They must be given a pension for the job they did for more than thirty to forty years of their lives for this country. For this, I have crafted the Universal Basic Income For Founders (UBIF).

WE RECEIVE A PROGRESS REPORT FOR LKG STUDENTS BUT NOT AS VOTERS

While watching the election results, my father insisted there was no point as the results are all fixed based on the money and liquor they distributed before the polls closed.

Suddenly, my daughter called me and showed me her progress report card for parent perusal and signing. I wondered why we are not getting any progress card on the government we have elected.

The government should present its progress report at regular intervals to all voters. I have not seen any reliable report card from any government so far. Many times, I come across the buzzwords gross domestic product (GDP) of the country, which often said to be the measuring stick of the country's growth as quoted by many intellectual, political and top bureaucrats in their speeches or at news conferences.

Let's have a true analysis on how it really represents the country's growth.

My little daughter pointed out of the slow-moving train and said, "Dad, you are a liar."

I asked, "Why?"

"You always insist I drink the water only from the RO plant but here they are collecting the water from small ponds. Health problems do not come for these places too?"

Perhaps nobody in India can give a convincing answer to this question.

Coffee is Rs. 200 in a 5-star hotel whereas to define whether a person is poor or not, Rs. 38 is sufficient enough to be considered above BPL, what discrimination!

If the GDP or any other numbers are a real representation of the true development of the country and people, why does this situation still prevail in society after seven decades of independence? I think currently majority considers GDP (Gross Domestic Product) numbers as the main yardstick for measuring a country's growth. If I am not wrong, the growth is around 6% on average till date. I think, if the evil of corruption is absent, then it would have been beyond 10% annually. Is this right?

Adya: As per as my financial knowledge gained through all my years at college and work I can firmly say that it is the not at all an exact yardstick for measuring the country's growth. The growth of the GDP is certainly affected by the hand of the ruling government and what it wants.

VVSS: You mean to say that the government can manipulate and guide the GDP figure?

Adya: No, GDP depends on various factors in India. A few are complex and a few easy.

Let's have a mention of the simple definition of GDP:

"Gross domestic product (GDP) is the monetary value of all the finished goods and services produced within a country's borders in a specific time period."

There are two components in this definition:

1. Finished goods

2. Services

Here there is a specific and solid demand always available for most of the finished goods but production by manufacturing is a typical task. So far, the government has focused on and worked towards service development so that our GDP can have a substantial figure.

Take the example of the IT sector including BPO, through GDP numbers for the past twenty years have been hanging around 5–7, yet India has not been seen as a developed country. The reason behind this is it totally depended and concentrated on the service sector instead of manufacturing, that is, in finished goods.

If you consider the case of agriculture output and its contribution towards the GDP, it is another shocker to everyone. Our achievement is that we should be able to reduce by nearly 55% to below the present 20% over sixty-five years.

This is the reason that India is looking to other small countries to help fill Indian bellies. We are at the mercy of a few foreign companies if you consider the defense sector where India is the world's largest importer. I feel embarrassed by this. I would have been happier if "India was the world largest exporter of defense products." I can confidently say that it is worth expecting this from 125 crore people. We are solely dependent on others for our security.

I think if India does not wake up and work towards a better infrastructure for manufacturing and agriculture then nobody should even be shocked that we look at other country for our daily food needs.

This is the reason I never be believe GDP figures. I only believe in the sincerity and dedication of the government and how it approaches the development of the poor and the young.

VVSS: Now, I understood the prime motive in pushing the campaign "Make In India."

They really want to increase the manufacturing facilities and therefore get more revenue for the finished products and as a result increase in the GDP.

Adya: But presently, the growth is not elevated as everyone expected when this campaign started.

VVSS: Yes, you are right. But it has two reasons, I would like to point out. Primarily, the establishment of manufacturing facilities at a single site takes months to years. It is a very lengthy procedure and is not possible to establish overnight.

The government is putting its best efforts in to encourage the youth and various manufacturers across the globe to establish facilities as a part of their Start-ups in India initiative.

Till here, everything is good, but recently you have probably come across many newspaper articles projecting the status of many start-ups in India. They are shutting down. In my opinion, it is mainly corruption that hinders their progress in business. Perhaps, in pursuit of this aim, the government has taken a bold step by announcing the demonetisation and subsequently, a cashless economy.

Now I can be very satisfied by this decision for the betterment of our country. We should feel proud as soldiers. We should be ready to take on more struggles in the construction of our country and transform it in new ways.

Adya: But in India, we currently do not have any development index on which we can rely on. This is a big drawback in our Constitution in my opinion.

VVSS: I totally agree with you and do you know that I have had the same doubt since I started my MBA (Master in Business Administration). Initially what I thought was a lack of comprehensive knowledge or exposure to the economy. I had to be satisfied with the idea that this is beyond our capacity to understand and *mugged up* the formulas to secure a passing grade.

A constitutional amendment must be made for a people's development index (PDI), which considers the average financial parameters, the reach of education, social security, reach of healthcare and the reach of transparent administration.

Which in turn is an aggregate of the following factors that cover all the basic needs of a human being for a dignified life, that is, food, clothes, shelters, education and security. This is indeed the immediate obligation of the government.

Hi beloved reader,

I put forward the best of my thoughts since I need regular and realistic feedback from the government.

It is needed even globally as the hunger for power and money by a few people affected the whole of mankind's fundamental development. Every country boasts like it is a massive achievement if they move forward in the pursuit of nuclear superiority, missiles and defense technology. I have never seen any country hitting the headlines, full of pride, saying that "100 percent of my countrymen have been provided or facilitated with access to their fundamental needs and are forever at ease." Perhaps, no one may be able to see such a statement until the corruption, life with disturbed values and terrorism are removed forever.

In view of the above,

Do you want the progress report on the ruling government of your motherland and for your selection by casting a vote?

If yes,

Come and join me in crafting the best ways to prepare this progress report. It must be cost-effective and time-bound yet effective and realistic.

PART – IV

New India

UNIVERSAL BASIC INCOME/INVESTMENT (UBII)

Let me remind you that our constitution provided fundamental rights, and the same cannot be changed, even Parliament has very limited scope to do so. These start with;

Right to Equality

Right to Freedom

Right against Exploitation

Right to Freedom of Religion

Cultural and Educational Rights

Right to Constitutional Remedies

Right to Privacy

These rights should make India heaven so people can live happily with a good social structure. However, due to increased differences in financial status, availability of modern infrastructure and politics, the word "equality" seems in danger.

In order to balance the differences, after Independence a few governments introduced numerous welfare schemes. These are being run across the country either by the central or state government or in partnership. However, there is no substantial change or development in the lives of core groups concerned, that is, the pillars of India, mother and infant, unemployed youth, care of the old, disabled and farmer (feeding god).

There is a great bias and discrimination in treating these groups due to independent states governing these groups. Some states gives good treatment to all whereas some states make these people live poor and humble lives producing the threat of increased inequality.

The hurdle these groups face, portrayed in previous parts, needs to be addressed with insight and equality across India. Recently, the government has started many national schemes and hope to equal everyone. One of the concepts gaining attention is UBI and JAM framework.

However, it is believed that these schemes need further customisation with some of the new concepts like mini-bank, IPay, etc to make effective implementation and within easy reach of the targeted group.

The scheme born out of this is "Universal basic income/investment (UBII)." It involves zero discrimination based on region or other aspects, and therefore, complete abolition of corruption.

It has 5 components that consist of 3 income and 2 investment groups:

- UBIM (Universal Basic Income for Mothers)
- UBID (Universal Basic Income for Disabled)
- UBIV (Universal Basic Income For Veterans)
- UBIF (Universal Basic Investment For Farmers)
- UBIY (Universal Basic Investments for Unemployed Youth)

It is designed to treat the concerns of these core groups in a more equal and responsible way across India under the framework of JAMI.

Adya: what is this JAMI environment?

VVSS: JAMI stands for Janadhan in mini/conventional banks, A-Vault, Mobile with IPay.

Janadan in mini/conventional banks means everybody should have the account. A-Vault, mandated linkage of their Aadhaar number to every financial transaction like linking to all his bank accounts, shares etc (this is covered in part III), and thirdly, mobile payments should be carried out with unique IPay on every mobile. This framework ensures no place for unlawful financial transactions like bogus transactions, fund transfers, loan evasion, etc. This surely gives the boost to the current central government drive like digital India, Swachch Bharath, DBT-direct benefit transfer, etc.

1. UBIM – Universal Basic Income For Mothers

The basic aim is to assist a lady who lost her wages upon taking the responsibility of motherhood till the child completes primary schooling. With this assistance, she can look after herself and the baby in her womb, later in her lap and in her house by grooming her kids with good values so they grow up energetic and responsible.

No substantial support is given to helpless women, except for a one-time lump sum amounting to Rs. 1000 or 9000 depending upon the state government. The Indian government gives them Rs. 6000 in three installments as part of a recently launched maternity benefit scheme. However, the optimum utilisation of this money is questioned along with the chance that it reaches the targeted person with the current banking and administration.

UBIM, My dear friends, I have one question. Why does any regular pregnant female employee need paid leave for 6 months? This is implemented by the government as an obligation for all organisations. But why does the same government never implement a similar policy for a wage-worker or other women working in the unorganised sector?

UBIM ensures regular monetary assistance to the women who just left a job due to the added responsibility of motherhood. Along with the loss of her daily wage, she is in need of extra nutrition and other health care, therefore, the financial requirement is higher (Detailed justification given in part III).

How much minimum income should she get and how long it should be issued and whom should be issued are three big questions that need to be addressed. Do you have any other kind of estimation, what you say Adya?

As per the Mr C Rangarajan committee, the minimum daily expenditure is above Rs. 32 in rural areas (Rs. 47 rupees in urban areas) and this is considered to determine the ones social status as above or below poverty line (BPL). The second consideration is that the wage of the husband is assumed to continue so the income for the family is not stopped completely but halved. The third consideration is the enhanced requirement of nutrition and health care during and post pregnancy.

I feel Rs. 1000 per month (32*30=960 so rounded to 1000) should be given to women on becoming a mother or on the verge of becoming one.

Secondly, it is justified if you raise your eyebrows about the effectiveness and success of this plan as similar schemes have failed and becomes a burden in some countries.

People might ask questions like:

- Who should be given the amount?
- How long should it be given for?
- How much should it burden the budget?
- Am I right?

I am sure that if this is completely customized and with technological advancements, those who are really in need will benefit. With the framework of the JAMI, it is very easy to verify facts like how much wealth is piled on her and her husband, if her husband has a fair earning to compensate the loss of wage from the wife, etc.

You also can consider other criteria and the category of the women decides if there is a burden on the budget.

The government has already included this into the budget for the maternity benefit program. Every pregnant woman receives Rs. 6000 in three installments to cope with the enhanced expenses.

But in our plan, every pregnant woman will be given Rs. 1000 every month for one year and later Rs. 500 rupees per month for a period of 5 years. This is under the assumption that after lactation period of one year she get back to work but earns reduced wage as the case of Smt Devi. The child also gains some strength. This responsibility should be shared by the government. Based on this fact, I propose the assistance of Rs. 500 is for 5 to 8 years.

Benefit to women, post motherhood, no more gloomy faces are caused by the loss of minimum wage. Now, she can look forward to healthy nutrition and can bring up her child in the healthiest way. This will surely be a huge benefit to the government. She can fulfill the basic responsibility of motherhood and need not fear expenses. The confidence of "she" will be more then "he" in the Indian family set up. Where so far no value for the she, especially in the BPL families though she earns equally.

The basic responsibility of the government is now fulfilled as there is a reduction in the infant mortality rate and a reduction in pregnancy-related deaths. Currently, India's total maternity mortality rate is 174 per 1 lakh births, which forms 17% of such deaths globally. This will surely be a huge benefit to the government.

So many governments desperately dream of making women more and more empowered. However, if their wish is real, they should feel more joy with this unique scheme with JAMI since their dream is achieved.

The exact financial implication on the Indian budget is not presented. However, it will be made available online and in the next edition of this book, until then, you can calculate with your own logic and formulas and share with us.

2. UBIY – Universal Basic Investment For Youth (Unemployed)

I need to remind you of one common saying by elders in families that all members should be treated equally and suitably. Let us seek clarification;

"Why are the youth from the same country not being treated equally? At some places there is an environment conducive to self-development and growth, elsewhere the environment is quite oppressive or there is no hope of gaining any support or skills?"

It's really shocking and painful to mention that every hour, one student commits suicide in India, according to 2015 data (the latest available) from the National Crime Records Bureau (NCRB). India has one of the world's highest suicide rates for people aged 15 to 29, according to the 2012 Lancet report. These suicides take place due to financial distress, along with many other causes, in my opinion. Shall we allow these numbers to continue despite our ability to help?

Aim Is to assist the youth with unemployment to meet daily needs like food so that they can concentrate on acquiring more skills or knowledge instead of being worried about earning for his bread and butter. In this process, some resorts to quick earning through terrorism, Naxalism, robbery, etc like Krishna in part III.

So many young people may not get the skills needed during formal academic classes to gain regular employment anywhere to prove themselvesin this world. The poor financial status at his home compels him to give up his dreams and end up in low-paying work or be exploited by miscreants. Is not right, Adya?

Presently, no such schemes are in the implementation stage across India equally. However, in some parts of India, independent states have similar schemes implemented successfully (only God knows when they will be really be rolled out). The benefit to the youth ranges from Rs. 120 per month to Rs. 9000 per month and again it depends on the state they belong to. The bias seen is shocking. In one state, one day's food expenses is given in the name of monthly allowance and in others, they give amounts almost equal to the salary of regular employment. Do you feel justified? Imagine the differences towards same youth in same country.

UBIY, the basic responsibility of the country's government is to ensure that the next generation is not treated with bias by providing assistance. If this trend continues, the divide will grow with a clear line of separation instead of it becoming one nation.

Under the scheme of UBIY, upon leaving college without any job or any regular employment, every unemployed youth will get a substantial interest-free loan at a staggered rate as a monthly grant for a certain period (3 years as per as my opinion, what do you say?) to meet his daily physiological and educational needs.

This is intended to equalize the assistance to all unemployed youth in the country and work against discriminatory assistance.

This truly supports the claim 'one needs to endeavour to ensure the younger generation is brilliant if one desire for them to produce a bright future for the country.'

Implementation and its financial implication on budget: I feel it is quite viable and offers more returns in the form of highly-brilliant youth for a new India. Since every person who opts for this plan can put in their best effort to get the job of his dreams and later, on attainment of this job, this money can be recovered from his earnings till the complete recovery of the loan.

Secondly, here it is an investment for the government not a gift like the current case of a free grant of thousands of rupees which never comes back to the exchequer.

Thirdly, you may have doubts about the recovery. How can the individual be tracked? This is very easy with the JAMI framework and absolutely no chance of escape or evade. Isn't it?

Now, more and more youth feel their life can be secure and they become more productive. No feeling of inferiority is seen among the youth who have unfortunately been deprived of quality education, access to basic physiological needs due to an absence of a supportive infrastructure and economical set up. This will reduce the trend of joining anti-social groups. In conclusion, they are more confidence and productive.

3. UBID – Universal Basic Income for the Disabled

We see the suffering of many healthy people in our life due to unemployment and the burden of the finances. What would be the degree of suffering and humiliation in the life if the same healthy people became disabled? Personally, this is very hard to even imagine.

What would be the situation in the case of those disabled since birth and discarded by their family? I think this situation is un-parallel to any kind of the struggle and demeaning.

Fortunate enough being human, since we are the only ones capable of taking care of our fellow beings. Consequently, the government is fortunate enough to offer substantial assistance in the form of income to meet the disabled person's needs.

In figures, as per the 2011 census, the total number of people with a disability stands around 2.68 Cr. Out of this, the males number 1.5 Cr and 1.18 Cr are female. Shockingly, a majority live in rural areas, that is, 69%.

After many decades of independence, we are leading to become signatory of few international forums, such as the enactment of the Persons with Disabilities Act, 1995. It comes with the objective to create an enabling environment to ensure equal opportunity, equality, social justice and employment of persons with disabilities.

The government even considered the UDID project to issue a unique identity card so that these groups can be reached and administrated without any fraudulent activity. These measures enhanced the confidence in these groups in terms of social and financial issues but not as expected. Therefore, administration of these must be easy and reachable. Some schemes need to see their last days as they have become ineffective and cumbersome. Do you agree Adya?

With the evolution of the technology over time, we must now look at each and every person with a disability (POD) with equal sight, opportunity and equal participation. Therefore, recently enacted "Rights of persons with disability act 2016," which is an enhanced version of previous acts it replaced. Maximum states are regularly providing disability pensions with some amount but not equally across India.

UBID, Under this plan every unemployed or low earning person must be given a monthly income as long as suitable employment is not gained. In most cases, it is required for life since many do not have the mental or physical capacity to gain any employment.

It may not be an extra burden on the exchequer since all the states have been issuing a substantial and monthly income to all eligible people.

Indeed, thousands of crores could be saved with the JAMI infrastructure since fraud and leakage of the funds will be completely erased. Equality is promised with an equal and streamlined stipend across the country. Further, the numerical analysis will be provided in the next edition. Do your calculations for justification and easy understanding of this plan.

With the technology-assisted UBIH scheme, every handicapped person will feel equal and socially secure. Equal and minimum funds are guaranteed to each and every eligible person to meet their daily requirements. With the ease of implementation, more rural areas are covered.

4. UBIV – Universal Basic Income for Veterans

Aim is to provide the minimum income to veterans who lost strength and energy in serving our nation. They must be respected in all the ways they deserve. Nowadays, many courts and governments frequently pass guidelines and enact new stringent acts to protect the rights of the elderly in society. This is very shameful if we are not able to fulfill their minimum needs, as they become weak and old by serving ourselves, therefore we currently enjoying the taste produced out of their sweat in the form of modern and safe environment. You must remember that later we will also soon be reaching that stage.

Presently, every ministry is trying their best to support our elders wherever possible. They have provided tax benefits, separate queues and appropriate reservations, etc. However, we have millions of old people and a majority reside in rural areas, nearly 71 percent. They cannot avail these facilities except the Indira Gandhi National Old Age Pension Scheme (IGNOAPS) (formerly known as the National old age pension scheme-NOAPS till 2009) by The Ministry of Rural Development, under which all aged above 60 get a monthly pension ranging from Rs. 200 to Rs. 1000 depending on their age and state government.

UBIF is similar to the current schemes but differs in terms of implementation which ensures zero corruption. Therefore, zero leakage and the most eligible elders are automatically assured it in the framework of the JAMI. It mandates universal and equal pension to all in the country, no more difference based on the residing states.

In the aspects of budgetary burden, perhaps, there will even be a small savings for the government due to the ease of implementation with complete transparency and replacing many schemes all over country.

Old age dependency ratio measures the number of those above 60 years as a share of those aged 15 to 59 years (working age). Currently, India has a ratio of 14.25% as per the population census 2011. It means nearly every 7 working aged person takes the responsibility of one elderly person. And for your information, Japan has the highest number with 35.1% in 2010, which means every 2.8 personnel has to take the load of one elderly person. If it increases for any country it burdens the financial system so difficult to implement the pension schemes. And we are fortunate enough that we are below the average of the world and other big nations.

As per the various census, nearly 40% of old people still work or are economically independent and the remaining 60% are dependent on others and institutes.

Thirdly, with the JAMI framework, we can very easily find out whose children have handsome earnings and are not supporting them so they can be forced to follow the law enacted on various occasions by the Indian government.

These three factors will definitely help figure out the real number of people in need of assistance.

Presently, assistance is given by the center and states in partnership towards pension. Out of which center contributes Rs. 200/- per month to people above 60 years and @ Rs. 500/- per month to persons those above

80 years belonging to from a household below the poverty line. Which is meant to be supplemented by at least an equal contribution by the States. But again this differs across states. However, few states pass same bucks to the old age without any contribution and few grants 5 times mores. This is discrimination, right? In conclusion, these figures are self-explanatory and show there is a lot of inequality and bias exists in the country. It has to be abolished with immediate effect as the implementation is not drawing any extra burden on the budget. Indeed, the situation offers savings upon implementation.

5. UBIF – Universal Basic Investment For Farmers

"Invest farming\... save feeder."

This universal basic investment is to pro-actively assist every helpless farmer in bringing every yard of his land to the status of farming without any fear of losing capital by the states and centre in partnership.

This scheme unquestionably increases the country's agricultural output and controls deaths of the feeding god (the farmer), potential to reduce the deaths from the current suicide rate of 11–13 percent. Our feeding gods, 13000 to 18000 of them, take their lives due to the burden of loans and other issues created by the failed output of cultivation. These silent deaths should be stopped and make farming the most preferred profession among the upcoming generation.

After witnessing so many disastrous incidents, natural calamities, drought and crop losses that led to suicides, every union government including independent states have introduced many schemes giving away billions of Indian rupees annually in the form of loan wavier, subsidised fertilizers and seeds. However, leaving bare minimum improvement, no scheme holds good for long for the entire arena of Indian farmers and other entities like banks, private money lenders, benami farmers, etc have benefited from these schemes.

Ironically, the farming sector must thrive for many to generate black money and divert it to various investments. This is the only sector that enjoys the absolute tax holiday forever so the generation of any amount of revenue from crops is free from any kind of tax. Many have stated farming is a good investment for the profit. It does not applicable to the genuine farmer but only hold true for high profile binami farmers who can withstand some blow and can bargain with the government and banking agencies for enough compensation.

Take the case of the crop loan, where hardly any poor farmer gets the loan due to the lengthy process and lobbying in the banks (detailed explanation presented in part III). It is again fully beneficial for benami farmers who avail the loan in lumpsums and divert it to other businesses. The real farmer is left empty-handed in desperation, which subsequently leads to suicide. Everybody question that why farmer should take the life instead of exploring other ways to sustain the life when farma business is not profitable? perhaps this is your opinion to, Adya?

My conviction is that they are not like corporate who are mastered in compensating the losses with the profit of the other business, even few are so smart enough in running away from the paying the debits to the banks and other lending institutes. These helpless farmers purely relay on only one business which full of the uncertainties, consequent to the low or nil output from the farma cultivation, sustainability is sometimes clueless. Now they have only two choices either to keep the hunger for the long or taking the life as preferred.

The above shocking facts take place due the current model of Government Political Corporate Banks Farm Assistance Model (GPCBFAM)

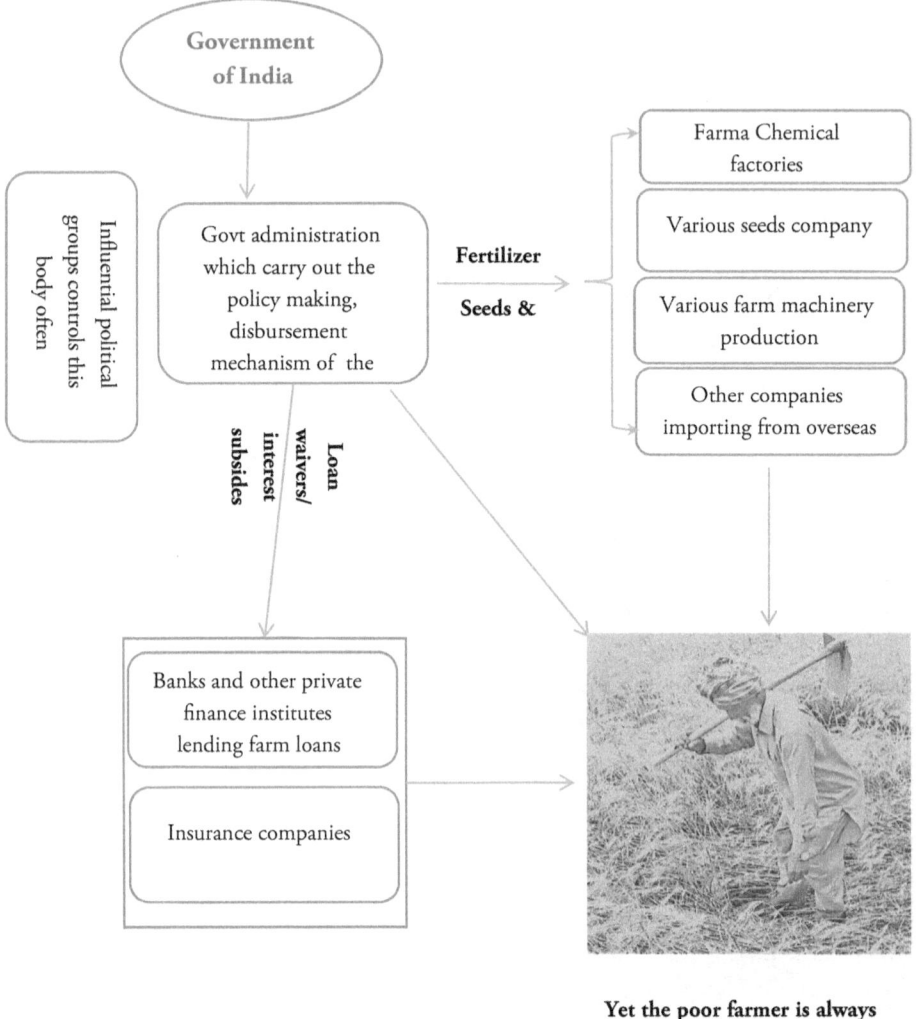

Yet the poor farmer is always in distress, sometimes this leads to suicide

Universal Basic Investment For Farmer (UBIF), this is a combination of the three current schemes "Agricultural Loan-Insurance -Loan Waiver."

These schemes urge the government to act proactive by investing in farming instead of loan-waiver and bailout package/compensations after disasters. Hereafter, in this scheme, every harvest is backed by government funding and confident farmer sweat. This is like business with a public-farmer venture.

This scheme guarantees high agricultural output and a high contribution to the national GDP with zeroing corruption and NPAs in the banking/other financial sectors which have been funding agriculture so far. As a result, it reduces the farmer suicides in India and increases development and education in rural areas.

In this scheme, the government will invest initially in every crop by providing unconditional credit to each farmer's special account called Kisan Investment Card (KIC) maintained by rural mini-banks (covered in part III). The amount is in proportion to the land owned or borrowed for farming. This card account is linked to three numbers: the farmer's savings account, the Aadhaar card and the land passbook number.

This credit will not be available for withdrawal. This is only useful for purchasing farming material. All farming vendors should have the facility to accept these credit cards and this is not a big issue since every vendor usually has a bank account and a basic mobile.

After the yield reaches home, the farmer does two things - one is to retain enough grain for their consumption and secondly sell the rest of the grain. Liquidation of the agricultural output, must preferably made through government agencies or government recommended buyers who offer reasonable prices and payments should be made through e-ways (IPay) to have prompt debit clearance and therefore interest bonus and tax holiday. Moreover, they can get prompt credit facility for the next harvesting cycle.

In simple words, this works like a normal credit card issued by the banks but it is issued by the government of India through mini-banks and the billing cycle is of a single harvesting period (usually 6 months).

Whenever the output is below average due to unwanted events like natural and man-made disasters, what would the consequences be and how would they handle the outstanding bills? Definitely this is your next question. Right?

Simple. It is like a joint venture between the public and farmer. Any losses incurred due to unexpected events will be waived by the government partially or fully. The main feature of this is to eliminate the current process of fake claims of losses.

THIS IS GOVERNMENT POSTAL FARM ASSISTANCE MODEL (GPFAM) BASED ON THE UBIF

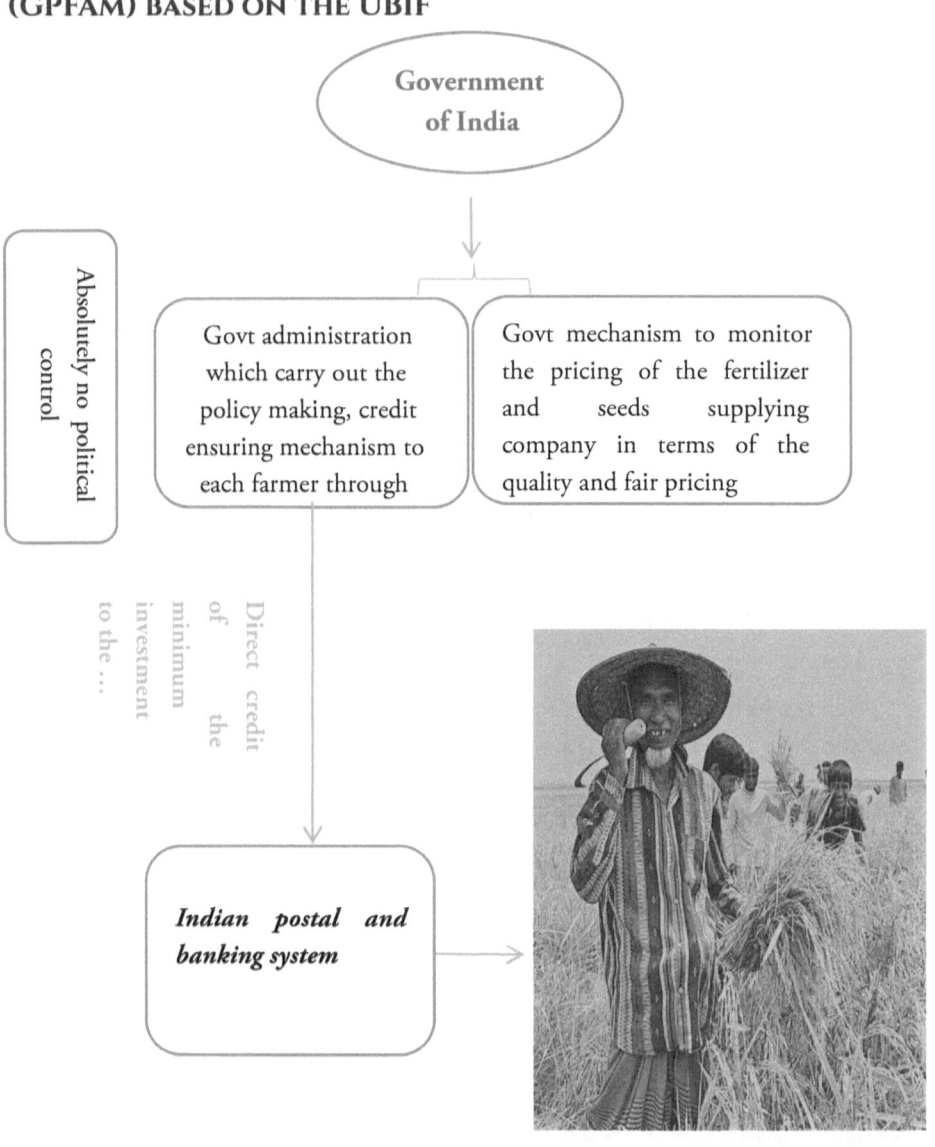

Government of India

Absolutely no political control

Govt administration which carry out the policy making, credit ensuring mechanism to each farmer through

Govt mechanism to monitor the pricing of the fertilizer and seeds supplying company in terms of the quality and fair pricing

Direct credit of the minimum investment to the ...

Indian postal and banking system

Happy and confident farmer always looks for a good yield to keep his family happy. No tension

Currently, all poor farmers wishing to avail government loans are rushing multiple times to nearby banks to plead with the staff. They land up in embarrassing situations like loans are granted by grace of the staff not the government. Many cannot think of taking a loan due to a fear of rejection or the lengthy process that involves long travel, multiple visits, pleading, bribery, etc. Some may even take on the burden of elevated interest rates against loans taken from the greedy local financiers.

This is eliminated as all post offices are turned into the banks. No more multiple visits to far banks. He need not fear accidental pooling of the funds with other personal expenses as these credits can only be used for the purchase of farm input material.

No fear of mental and physical trouble from private and unauthorized local lenders.

Each and every aspect is monitored by the government so disbursement of funds is quick. Now they only think of the next cycle of harvest.

Benefits to the government and taxpayers: If we consider the aspects of benefits of the government and taxpayers, so far, the main headache of the government and banks is how to determine and disburse loans to genuine farmers. Now this is automatic as each mini-bank and SOFT handles the administration.

High GDP contribution even in natural calamities: All possible land comes under the cultivation with the UBIF. So there is substantial increase in the agricultural output.

In the case of natural calamities and other unwanted events, they can easily waive the proportionate loss in transparent and quick ways. Even the government can urge the farmers to go for any alternative crop for the period left in the current session of harvest. Absolutely no false claims, which saves thousands of the crores. Therefore, stopping the generation of black money.

Absolutely abolish mediator subsidies. Hereafter, there is definitely no need of giving away subsides to any entity. No financial and administrative burden in handling the subsidies for fertilizers and other seeds, etc. These schemes absolutely discourage subsidies and even ban any subsidies in India in the field of agriculture.

UBIF recommends all chemical and seed companies do their business as other businesses do. They can sell their product at reasonable prices. There is absolutely no leakage of subsidy funds. So lakhs of crores can be saved per year.

They only need a better price and quality monitoring body to arrest high prices for farming products. Since one bad quality seed can kill many farmers and their yield for the entire harvest.

No issue with NPA: Due to the strong, closed mechanism of disbursement of credit, no overdrawing is possible. The UBIF mandates liquidation of the agricultural output through e-payments in order to get tax benefits and to avail the credit for the next harvest cycle. So loans are automatically repaid if the output is sufficiently gained.

Full development of India is in sight, transforming from developing nation to developed nation. Every farmer will give his best, the contribution to the Indian GDP will improve and there will be happy families in rural areas.

FINANCIAL VIABILITY IN THE GOVERNMENT PROSPECT

Present loan per hectare by banks and other financial institutes in India:	50,000 to 70,000 Indian rupees (depend on the type of institute providing loan, climatic condition of the area whether it is coastal or drought prone, etc).
Share of the loan taken by a genuine farmer against the total agricultural loan presented by the banks	Only 35% of the total loans sanctioned reaches the farmer and the remaining reaches God only knows where... this is a shocking revelation by some news report.
Government subsidies for fertilisers and other farming chemicals as per the 2017 union budget	70,000 crores (700 billion) of Indian rupees annually
Total outstanding farm loan as on 2017 Total loan so far waived across India by independent states	Total estimated agricultural loan outstanding 3.1 lakh crores ($3100 billion) Indian rupees. And waived amount by various states Andhra Pradesh, Madhya Pradesh, Rajasthan, Punjab, Uttar Pradesh in aggregate is Rs. 1300 billion
Total expenditure in the form of the farm subsidies including fertilisers, interest free loans, loan waiver, etc (2016–2017)	In efforts to rescue farming sector and farmers, so far roughly allotted tax payer money is Rs. 25000 billion in the current year. The big question is – has this amount really helped the targeted sector and people?
Total NPA in the agri-loan:	20 to 30 percent of every bank's NPA are for agricultural and related loans. Do we really believe that these are from genuine farmers?
Total Indian land and land under cultivation	Total Indian land area is 3.287 million square kilometers 52.8 (arable land) + 4.2 (permanent crop) totaling to 57% of total India land is used for the cultivation as per Wikipedia and central intelligence agency fact book.

Total budget outlay for the purpose of the Kisan Credit scheme is Rs. 10 lakh crores as per the budget speech of the Indian finance minister. And also as per media reports, only 30% of this fund goes to farmers and the remaining? God only knows.

In this plan, even the government invests unconditionally in every acre of the arable land at the present rate of the loan; it should not be more than Rs. 7 lakh crores per year instead of the current estimation of 10. The management is very easy as investment is staggered through the harvest cycle and not in one sum. The recovery cycle starts after 6 months, which is the maximum gestation period for any crop.

In conclusion, I can proudly say that, with the UBIF, the Indian agricultural sector will definitely regain its old status and fall in line with the golden words of the legend George Washington

> "*Agriculture, Is the most healthful,*
> *most useful, and most noble employment of man*"

Hello reader friends,

Thanks for reading all of my book as it contains myself. Without you this book would perhaps not exist. I am grateful to endorse your ideas by featuring them in the next reprint or edition. Let us work together since your experiences and wisdom may give a more solid foundation to our endeavor to make a New India.

I am going to publish the next book titled Silent Murderers, which will have personal experiences about the environment, farming, and farmers handling India are included in the above stories.

SOFT

(Social and Financial Technical Apprenticeship)

Hello,

Where do you work right now? Is it a new or old office?

I was recently posted to a new place. In my new workplace, on the very first day I was approached by a co-worker. He asked me to look after his work and he would return soon from the bank as soon as his money was transferred to his home, which was located thousands of miles away. I stopped him and asked if he availed internet banking.

"Then, you need not rush to the bank every time for transactions. You can manage everything from your home."

His response was shocking. He quickly recollected many Online fraudulent incidents as reported by friends or stories in news. Further, he is not smart in handling Online transaction securely though postgraduate in Information Technology.

If this is the case with one postgraduate, what could be the situation of less educated or illiterate people whom you are asking to contribute towards the cashless economy by embracing online and mobile payment systems.

Of course, today's society has technology-driven management everywhere. We have to catch up with technology at least to the extent of our own daily lives. In other words, without technology our life is certainly sluggish.

The main cause behind this sluggish life is our current and past education system where the adoption of technology is limited. Perhaps, they never expected technology becomes predominated in human-life in coming days. As a result despite a fair formal education, we often end up confused by the management of day-to-day technology. I am sure you agree that half of educated people are still afraid to embrace technology or feel it is beyond their ability. Therefore, nobody looks for technology-driven solutions like net banking or using mobile payment systems.

And it is highly impossible to send everyone back to school to learn technology. Even if the almighty makes it possible, this is a waste of their time and resources as the need for technology varies from person to person.

Mere suggestion and a little guidance is enough for many people. Urban and semi-urban areas will get this assistance but the villages need more to manage their lives with technology. One or two smart student can help them but they will not be available every day. I would like to keep special people available for them for some time every day. They are called "social and financial technical apprentices" (SOFT Apprentices).

Presently, there is no such assistance available for the people of rural and semi-urban areas. Only available assistance is for administrative and revenue matters in the form of the president and village revenue officer.

In recent years, thanks to the Aadhaar-based authenticated system, many banks have deployed their representative to villages with micro-ATMs where villagers can carry out micro-fund transactions without travelling miles to reach the banks.

The aim of SOFT is toassist the rural people in day-to-day financial transactions, carry out field study and find suitable people to educate citizens about government financial assistance schemes.

SOFT is supposed to be conducted by the government and banks so that incumbent youth, government and banking will benefit from this.

Youth with a minimum qualification of graduation or diploma will be deployed to the village for a period of 12 months including initial training at the Mandala or District headquarters. The training in collaboration with the banking institutes may cover prevailing banking development, payment systems (IPay), mini-banking system in rural areas, Universal basic income/investment models, insight of government financial assistance/welfare schemes to various sections of people, farmers, potential educated and non-educated youth, etc. This course may be for two weeks. What do you say?

Upon completion of training, they will be allotted the necessary mobile and micro ATM to start work in the field. He will work in coordination with the rural mini-bank and other administrative staff for the betterment of villagers. He has to carry out field study and find suitable people to educate about the available government assistance schemes along with carrying out micro-financial transactions whenever villagers need it.

Definitely you are in agreement with me that, Lakhs of youth pass out annually from colleges and other institutes as the graduates and postgraduates without any real and practical environmental exposure of the subjects studied in class. This statements merits more in the case of rural, semi-urban and even a few from high profile colleges. Even after scoring a distinction in their studies they are not confident in the practical handling of the situations they already studied on.

Post leaving campus, many students fail to pursue further knowledge required to secure a permanent job due to time and financial constraints. These students can feel blessed by this plan as they can gain a substantial stipend, practical exposure and a valuable government issued certificate.

This is useful in designing their own career as this apprenticeship opens up their mind about several ideas which may lead to good and promising start-ups.

In the lives of rural population, so far nobody is around to educate, motivate and assist their financial development. They can now start cashless transactions fearlessly as the assistance/first hand customer-care is available next door in the form of SOFT. Indeed, this becomes a lifeline to the modern way as one dedicated person is being deployed for assisting every financial need. The energetic youth will have consultation with villagers for finding areas that require assistance.

Government will now be able to provide training (both theory and practical) and employment to youth on a large scale. They can reach every man of India with their sincere work and financial welfare scheme through SOFT apprentice. The reach of government financial schemes will now be widespread and to genuine beneficiaries.

The government and banks can recruit these SOFT for permanent jobs in their offices. After familiarisation with banking, financial schemes and field experience they can give best from the first day of employment. Alternatively, they may venture into a start-up using their experience. The government should place a provision of considering SOFT as an extra merit whenever incumbents apply for government financial allied departmental jobs.

If the youth are supported and therefore, so are the rural population then everybody can easily conclude that the country will become the most developed and strong country on this planet.

Voters Progress Report

PEOPLE DEVELOPMENT INDEX (PDI)

For the past couple of years, there has been a dramatic change in the development and the transparency level of the administration. There has also been an image makeover at the international stage.

Yet can we say we are at the developed state we are supposed to be at after seven decades of Independence? For me, we are below the average standard of the life in developed countries. We are still at the lowest position in the fields of manufacturing linked to defense, electronic chip technology, etc.

Here, no government can take all the blame since, every government did some work towards the betterment of this country. As a result, the RTI act and Aadhaar have taken birth in India. However, in my opinion, these are building blocks for India and lay the rigid foundation stone for transparent governance, uplifting the poor in India and thus, the eradication of corruption which obviously promises a conducive atmosphere for any kind of business.

So far there is no provision nor any method to reflect the exact development index, especially in diverse countries like India. The index like GDP (Gross Domestic Production), NDP (Net Domestic Production), Trade Deficit and other financial indexes does not realistically reveal the financial and social status of the poor.

Had these indexes been of true real relevance to the development of the common man and his environment, there should not be any concern regarding the bad air quality in the capital, soaring temperature levels in the city of Bangalore which once used to be considered a pleasant and healthy city, there should not be any deaths due to lack of the basic health assistance, no instance of patients being carried on others shoulders to the far-flung hospitals, no instance of women delivering their babies by the road or in hospital corridors; it is unfortunate to have this incident in India after 70 years of independence. India must be at the same level as other counties where they proudly boast high GDP numbers.

There must be a new index which should be measured and projected periodically, may be annually or bi-annually. This reporting should not be more than bi-annually so that every government has to present at least 4 or 2 progress report to the voters.

What do you say, Adya?

Adya: Earlier, I came across the few index what you expected to be. The Human Development Index (HDI) developed by Indian economist Amartya Sen and Pakistani economist Mahbub ul Haq as a part of United Nations Development Program (UNDP). Presently India stands at the 131st position in the world.

VVSS: Yes, I know this, but I personally questions the influence of this index on our system. Therefore, a more elaborative, customized index system must be in place for this great diverse India.

To formulate the index by which everyone should be able to understand the functioning the of government and the average living status of India in terms of food, shelter, social security, income levels, access to quality health and education, and transparency level of governance.

Every human being on this planet needs these basic things – 1. Air 2. Water 3. Food 4. Shelter 5. Health 6. Education 7. Social status and security. These are only possible if all the resources in the country are managed efficiently with a transparent mechanism called good governance.

The progress report should not be more than a single (A4) size paper and all are summered up with a single index.

Basis for calculation may be formed with the help of the current index:

1. GDP
2. Net agriculture product
3. Literacy rate including the High school, beyond the graduation.
4. Unemployment rate
5. Population below Poverty line
6. Trade deficit 1 (International market imports and exports, and importing basic food commodities like rice, wheat, pulses and vegetables like onions, tomato, have a very negative impact on the index, since we are not self-reliant at least in securing what our bellies need)
7. Trade deficit 2 (this is excluding the above mentioned)
8. Green cover ration deforestation and forestation
9. Water secured for farming by constructing dams
10. Health index includes child mortality rate, life expectancy, average distance for access to the primary health centers

People Development Index (PDI), this index, also has a vital role for a well-performing government in the subsequent election. They cannot prepare exhaustive, sometimes un-realistic manifestoes to lure the innocent. This index gives everyone rough figures so they can decide easily before voting. Henceforth, voters are on par with LKG students in getting a progress card for their approval.

VOTER PROGRESS CARD: PEOPLE DEVELOPMENT INDEX*

FIELD	COVERDE ASPECTS	Achieved score (for 100 marks)	Weightage based final score	Total score
Agri yield and prices	Rice, wheat, other pulses and vegetables	55	10	550
Atmosphere	Air quality, forest cover etc	33	05	165
Health	Life expectancy, Infant mortality rate, maternity mortality rate, average distance to nearby community health center, number of the community centers per 1 lakh population	66	15	990
Education	Literacy rate, Unemployment youth rate, average school distance, teachers and student ratio, etc	45	15	675
Overall production	GDP	55	10	550
Unemployment rate	How many youth without any kind of earning and availing UBIY	60	10	600
Ratio of BPL		70	10	700
Trade deficit 1	Basic food and material	55	05	275
Trade deficit 11	Excluding materials mentioned above	55	05	275
Corruption	Corruption index	66	05	330
Rural infrastructure	Roads, electrification, drinking water, Telecommunication etc	55	10	550
People development Index PDI (out of 100)				56.6

* Above PDI model is best out of all type of "Voters Progress Card" models from the authors work. however, if you have better one which projects real all- round development at ground level in lives of people. your are most welcomed to feature your model here in next edition on your name.

Adya: The question worth a trillion is "Was demonetisation a hit or miss?." This is still under debate and its answer is under evolution at various levels by various people across the globe.

So far you are rating and seeking to rate the government with a progress card, You tell me, what is your overall score for demonetisation?

VVSS: There is Newton's third law of motion "For every action, there is an equal
(laughs) and opposite reaction." He did not or perhaps could not mention what is the delay in the reaction, so that some big action may not have a conclusive reaction immediately. However, I will explain.

As per as my opinion, this remains to be the most historic step seen in India. Leaving bad or good effects aside, it changed this society and everyone's life. Whether they were elite or a beggar, this move rapidly pushed through to all the corners of the banking system and digital payment platforms. Until then nobody might have ever thought of the importance of banking in their life and in a country's financial set-up.

It provides various opportunities for many citizens and institutes to correct their respective financial conduct to prove they are clean and to keep themselves effective. Many become responsible citizens by declaring unaccounted assets, income and paying tax. The tax nest is consequently extended, which in turn boosts the revenue of the country so there is easy administration of social welfare schemes.

Banking was able to figure out its mismanagement on all fronts. Investigation agencies and tax collection system are now able to work effectively with reduced illegal activities in all sectors like black/fake currency circulation etc. However, I admit that the continuation of this effect is in question with the current financial and banking set-up.

For the government, it was a monumental step involving equal degrees of administration. During this phase, it certainly taught many lessons, so they can be more proactive in governance in the ages to follow. As it happened in the age of technology, this is going to be last act of demonetisation on such a large scale in Indian history. The next generation may not see the need of demonetisation as we are moving rapidly towards the cashless economy. The entire world even admitted the positive impact of this move. Few international agencies enhanced their credibility by revising their outlook to positive side; like IMF and world bank upgraded Indian status in ease of doing business. Recently Moody's rating, which is internationality accepted, a Credit Rating Agency based in USA, too enhance the rating after the gap of 13 years.

On the flip side, as we witnessed, the common man was forced all of sudden through a terrific level of hardship. We saw when any big decision is planned nation-wide, covering all sections of people, so many political and administrative aspects come under play. I think, the time of demonetisation is perfectly suited. However, implementation should have been more well-planned with extended ground work done by the RBI and public service providers like railways. It is worth mentioning here that whether the country's financial goals were achieved or not, the hopes of the common man should be fulfilled sooner or later. Otherwise this will remain the worst disaster in India history.

Finally, it also stimulated us so that we could discuss and produce so many solutions for the problems we experienced. Similarly, others might have similar thought processes, so let us urge everyone to come up and join with us in building a New India.

I wish you good luck in building a new India for future generations... "Dare to dream."

Thank you.
with lot of blessings from you...
Temporally signing off

Adya and VVSS
vvssprasad@outlook.com

Annexure: ONE INDIA ONE CURRENCY ONE PAYMENT SYSTEM (IPAY)

is to stream line the digital payment system across the India by bringing beggar to billionaire on single platform with the unique framework which works on every mobile/computing devices with or without internet and for every sum of payments in ever safest way on the single line

"*one India*

one currency

one payment system"

Presently there are multiple payment systems, non have the wide base to cover every section of the people as well as every range of transactions. Adaptability is difficult for anyone. I think, enough discussion made over the disadvantages in part II of this book. *However for understanding, providing technical details of current popular payment systems NEFT, IMPS, WALLET Services, USSD based IMPS, RTGS, AADHAAR Pay.*

RTGS: Real time gross settlement, is the one of the oldest and still being in use payment system. As on 1985, three central banks had implemented RTGS systems, while by the end of 2005, reached to 90 central banks of various countries.

This system typically used for high-value transactions that require and receive immediate clearing. Transfer of money or securities takes place from one bank to another on a "real time" and on a "gross" basis. Settlement in "real time" means a payment transaction is not subjected to any waiting period, with transactions being settled as soon as they are processed. "Gross settlement" means the transaction is settled on one-to-one basis without bundling or netting with any other transaction. "Settlement" means that once processed, payments are final and irrevocable. RTGS payments typically incur higher transaction costs and usually operated by a country's central bank. *It works only during the bank working hours only.*

NEFT: Nation electronic fund transfer, Reserve bank of India introduced in Sep 2005 and State bank of India is the first bank to implement. However, made availability to wide customer base through online as a part of their internet banking services by ICICI and HDFC and other private banks. Bank customers in India can transfer

Annexure: One India One Currency One Payment System (IPay)

funds between any two NEFT-enabled bank accounts on a one-to-one basis. It is done via electronic messages. Fund transfers through the NEFT system do not occur in real-time basis. All fund transfer requests are bundled, cleared in hourly (half hourly now) batches with 12 settlements occurring between 8:00 AM and 7:00 PM on bank working days. Transfers initiated outside this time period or on bank holidays are settled at the next available window. This service is not instant, not free, limited amount from 1 ruppes to 10 lakh rupees only. This fact alone obviously stands defeated in facilitating everyone s needs of fund transaction. This transaction can be carried out at branch, online internet banking, few of banking apps only.

IMPS: *Immediate Payment Service*, this is one of instant and real-time inter-bank electronic funds transfer system through mobile phones in India. Unlike NEFT and RTGS, the service is available 24/7 throughout the year including bank holidays.

It is managed by the National Payments Corporation of India (NPCI) and is built upon the existing National Financial Switch network (NFSN). NFSN was designed, developed and deployed by the Institute for Development and Research in Banking Technology (IDRBT) in 2004, with the goal of inter-connecting all ATMs in the country. IMPS was publicly launched on November 22, 2010. The versatility of this service that it can be accessed through various platforms like banking internet site, apps, and USSD on basic phones. This is only system can run on basic mobile to access the banking.

E-WALLETS: For me, it is organized by non banking institutes like Paytm, mobikwik etc. Similar to the bank accounts. Though they gained momentum at rapid pace till recent time, these have it's own disadvantages due to the rules and regulation formulated by the company and central banks. They have the transaction capacity max 1 lakh per month in a account where KYC compliant otherwise limit is only 20000 per month. Another apprehension is that non compliant accounts are good channel for unaccounted money circulation. In user interface front, this service is only available through smart-phone app or web site. Not available for the low end devices.

AEPS: Now a days everybody hear in India that finger print with Aadhaar number are sufficient to make the payments and even withdrawal of money at the micro ATM usually possessed by the business correspondent of the banks. This Aadhaar enabled payment system (AEPS) empowers a bank customer to access his basic banking services with Aadhaar number and his finger print. The beauty of this system is that customer can carry out transactions like withdraw money from all his accounts from various banks at single Micro ATM like using other bank debit cards at the another bank ATM machine.

In conclusion,

> *I can, may be you as well, firmly convinced that current multiple payment systems are complex, have no potential to serve nationwide, with involvement of so many apps, and organization like banks, private NBFS etc. With emerge of new technology, few of these payment services should have been outdated by this time.*

IPay, This payment system is analogue and replacement to currently existing IMPS and AADHAR based payment system being in implementation on various platform in different ways by different agency.

Objects of this system, is not to have the new technology over the existing but to seek the uniqueness in the field of payment system.

Uniqueness: eases the adaptability universally. No more independent banking and payment apps. This is only one payment service for all people and institutes including for all banks.

Wide Equipment Compatibility: Makes everyone to use this service on any kind of device. In India, wide divergence exists in the mobile devices used by Indian population ranges from the basic mobile phone with only feature of calling to smart phones with 4th generation of internet speed supported.

Fastest Ever Payment Method with the Real Time Payment Settlement: Irrespective of banking and other institutes working timings. Your every transaction has to be full filled in real time No matter when you transact, what amount you transact, where you send.

Promising Financial Privacy and Ultimate Security: IPay is the unique feature of Multichannel Transaction Authentication Protocol (MTAP) (simultaneous use of USSD and internet channels) for high volume transactions along with multi layer security and authentication methods like OTP, Finger Print, Mpin, Device Registration Etc enables transactions without any limits, even with basic phone lakhs can be transferred safely. Since all are AADHAAR linked bank account and registered so 100 percent absent of proxy/middleman account manipulation. No chance of the fraud transaction ever.

Its architecture offers the best financial privacy by providing great flexibility. It completely discourages the AADHAAR number based transaction. It only accepts the either mobile number or virtual address to access account for transactions promising flexibility, since both can be changed whenever the user wish to do so.

Cheapest Payment Methods: as it can works with either internet or mobile communication. Costly payment swiping machines are replaced with tablet PCs with EMV chip readers/finger print scanners with enhanced user interface experience for both merchant and payer. Whose cost just around 4000.

Single Stop Customer Care for Entire India: Currently, on failed or pending transaction grievance redressal, multi-point approach is required to sort out the issues. One need to approach bank, on some other occasions bank asks customer to approach the merchant for grievance redressal. In the case of the IPay framework, single point of customer care. For rural and semi urban, in addition, they have the SOFT as primary point customer care.

Embed of Advance Technology: To enable rich experience it can embeds the NFC (Near field communication) and BLE (low energy Bluetooth) communication in case of physical store shopping.

Support of Anonymous Funding: In some case you need to fund anonymous to some institutes like political funding and charitable funding etc. It is designed to support such transaction keeping your identity under cover.

Forms Nationwide Network: This unique payment system seeks mandatory alignment by all banks, all merchants, all bill collectors like schools, telephone operators, tax, to form single and largest payment network

Incredibly Credible: This payment system is Governed by Govt. of India through RBI and being used by all section of people and institutions in the country.

Annexure: One India One Currency One Payment System (IPay)

IPay System framework

This system mainly divided into 5 modules to fit all kind of communication devices.

- Feature phone based
- Smart phone based

Tablet PC based for merchants (B2C and B2B)

- Smart wallet child cards
- Web based

All software modules will work on either of USSD/Internet channel with payment server computers providing communication flexibility. However With USSD channels selected, you may not able to cater all your requirements

Now You may doubt "I am aware of Internet on mobile but never heard about the USSD? Right!"

Unstructured Supplementary Service Data (USSD), sometimes referred to as "Quick Codes" or "Feature codes." and length of messages up to 182 alphanumeric characters long. It is a end to end session-based protocol mobile SMS (Short massage service) or real time SMS service over securely established communication channel. The communication channel remains open between mobile and service provider's server allowing continuous exchange of data and only terminates when either of party wishes to end the communication. For clear differentiation and reference, conventional SMS and MMS can be stored and sent to destination by telecom operator as and when destination number becomes live. But this can not be done with USSD as this requires both source and destination should be live simultaneous. For further you please refer relevant literature. Lets move to original topic.

This is, undoubtedly going to be a common gateway for all kind of payments including utility payment services across India. In other words, one would be able to pay any kind of bill payments, taxes, insurance premium on single click.

However, few explained concisely as they encounters for easy understanding.

Network topology of IPay frame work is provided on next page for elementary understanding. And, sample demonstration of "how this IPay works with Graphical User Interface (GUI) on Different Devices" in following pages. Necessary pictorial representation and comments provided on site for effortless understanding. Design accuracy and richness is compromised for easy representation.

Every bank should promote this app only for online transactions against present independent apps by each bank. This step certainly feels everyone equally experienced.

Annexure: One India One Currency One Payment System (IPay)

NETWORK TOPOLOGY

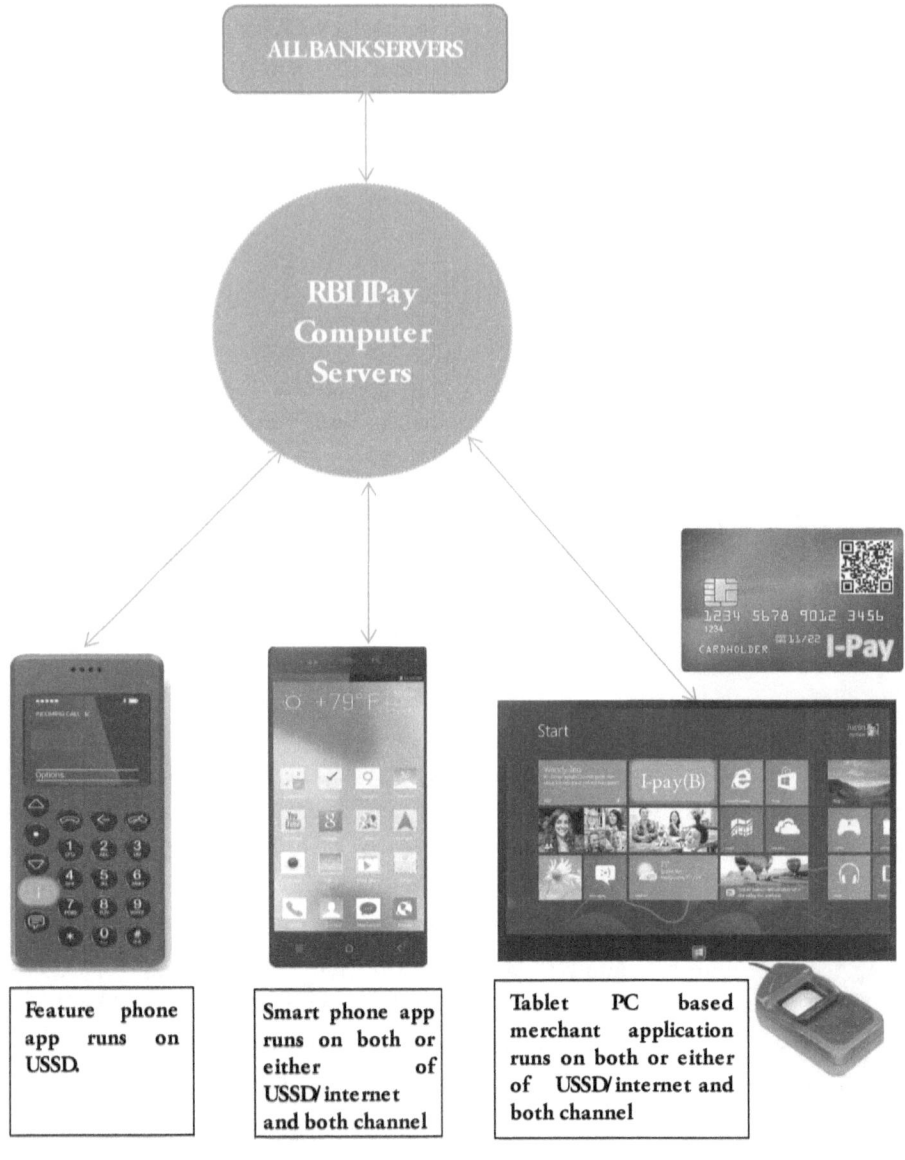

Annexure: One India One Currency One Payment System (IPay)

BASIC/FEATURE PHONE IPAY APPLICATION

Conditions

Every feature mobile including basic black and white screen mobile should have the IPay application pre-installed by the original manufacturer (OEM) as same as the basic apps like massaging and calling.

- Doubts may be raised that basic phones does not support the Graphic User Interface (GUI), therefore having this apps may not be feasible. In basic phones this app is same as the messaging app which is programmed to dial automatically required numbers like

TO SELECT LANGUAGE	TO SELECT BANKS
English *99#	Sbi *99*41#
Hindi *99*22#	Pnb *99*42#
Tamil *99*23#	Hdfc *99*43#
Telugu *99*24#	Icici *99*44#
Malayalam *99*25#	Axis bank *99*45#
Kannada *99*26#	Canara bank *99*46#
Gujarati *99*27#	Bank of india *99*47#
Marathi *99*28#	Bank of baroda *99*48#
Bengali *99*29#	Idbi bank *99*49#
Punjabi *99*30#	Union bank *99*50#
Assamese *99*31#	Central bank *99*51#
Oriya *99*32#	Still………..no ends

- These apps do not require any updation in later stages as these works in the USSD frameworks where no threat of any cyber crime like hacking activity.
- There must be legal frame work that every mobile selling in the India should come with IPay pre-installed. And if possible, hard-key/soft key in key board should be provided to launch app in one touch.
- Currently many banks and third party apps have designed this kind of apps without need of dialing these many codes. But all these apps again have the limited scope as these are only for the smart phone, and no authority.
- Only limitation of this IPay on feature phone is that it may not have the rich Graphic User Interface and high volume transaction beyond lakhs of rupees. Since it is assumed that only illiterate or poor villagers only uses the the basic phone.
- Specimen copy of app architecture is provided in following page and complete architecture will be made available online after all feedback received from all potential readers.

TO PAY/SEND MONEY....

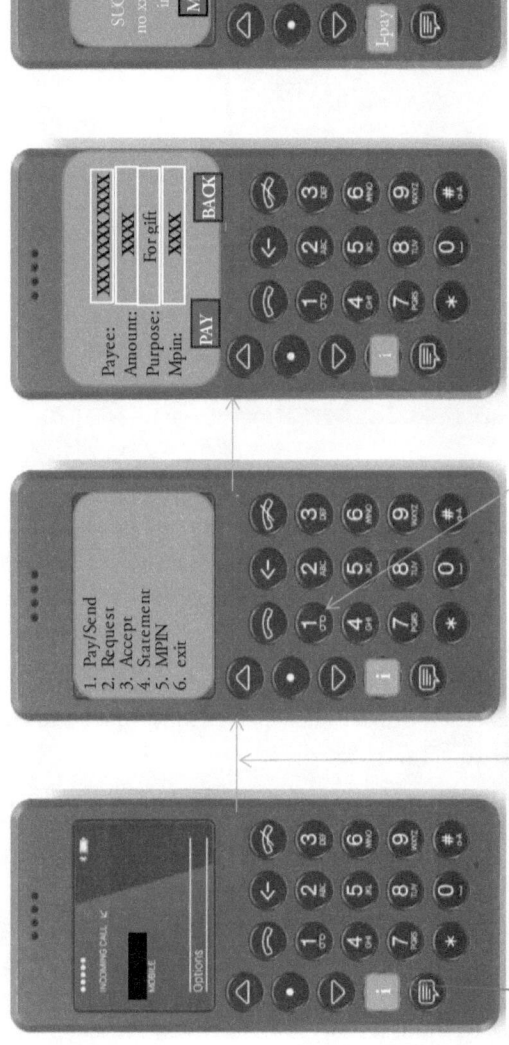

Press dedicated key for I-Pay App to launch directly

Select from menu in case of non availability of dedicated I-pay key on keypad to launch application

Select 1 For Payment/ Sending of Money

After entering payee /mobile no /merchant ID, amount, purpose of payment, Mpin, he will select pay option. sooner pressing this option, App should send this info on USSD massage.

Replay from the system server presenting the results of the transaction whether successful or fail. in case of success, then transaction reference and remaining balance in Account should appear

MAIN ADVANTAGE OF THIS APP IS TO COMPLETE ANY TYPE OF TRANSACTION IN *SINGLE CYCLE OF COMMUNICATION*. AND ABSENT OF DIALING MANY TIMES FOR SINGLE TRANSACTION AS IN THE CASE OF CURRENTLY FOLLOWED USSD FORMAT.

Annexure: One India One Currency One Payment System (IPay)

SMART PHONE IPAY APPLICATION

Conditions

Indeed, presently countless payments Apps are available for smart phones. Since this platform provides lot of space for developers to design and incorporate customized features in the apps as they wish. No space and process restriction in any way in this platform.

However, the only concern is that *security*. As everybody admits that this is comparably more vulnerable for data theft or hacking etc. This must first be addressed before allowing the crores of rupees to get transacted.

IPay for smart phone, is capable of running on three channel of communication.

Internet

USSD

Internet and USSD.

Last one needs to enable Multichannel Transaction Authentication Protocol (MTAP) (simultaneous use of USSD and internet channels) for high volume transactions, making authentication safest method in this world.

Annexure: One India One Currency One Payment System (IPay)

This app total 7 layers of the security and nearly impossibly to hack for anybody.

- *First level:* is device registration through app installed.
- *Second level:* Mobile number must be in the same mobile and registered.
- *Third level:* User ID,
- *fourth level:* the app Password/Mpin,
- *Fifth level:* Hug Transaction Password (which is not as usual, this password is entered in newly and automatically initiate USSD channel when the request for the high amount transfer is forwarded)
- *Sixth level:* Auto-detection of OTP.
- *Seventh-level:* every account is linked to the AADHAAR, results in the zero fake accounts.

Alas! How can anyone dare to initiate fraudulence transaction?

I think you may be wondering that These many layers may become tiredness in the user. Right?

All layers are needed when user wish to transfer hug amount in no delay (real time). however, necessary to explain: what are the layers are needs to be used when.

For amount below 10,000 is 3 layer in force (device verification, App password and MPIN is only required).

For amount above 10000 and below 100,000, is 5 layer in force (device verification, App password MPIN and extra two layer are, sim verification, OTP authentication by Auto SMS scanning for the OTP).

For amount above 100,000 is the 6 layers in force (along with previously methods, another is high transaction password in MTAP structure)

And it is to be noted that 7th layer is by default for all as all accounts are mandatorily linked to all accounts)

Specimen copy of app architecture is provided in following page and complete architecture will be made available online after all feedback received from all potential readers

TO PAY/SEND MONEY ..... WITH SMART PHONE....

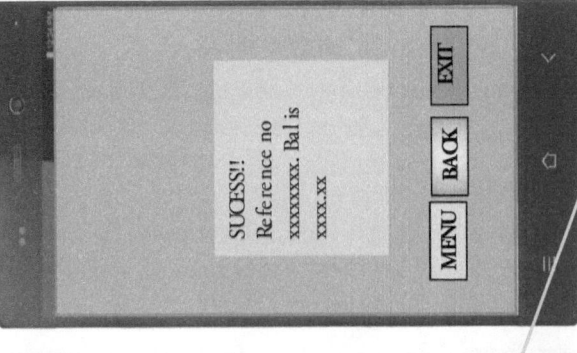

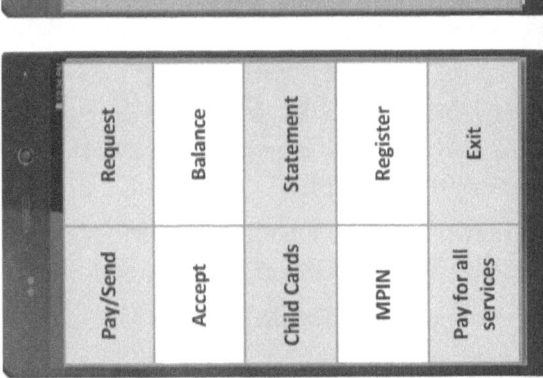

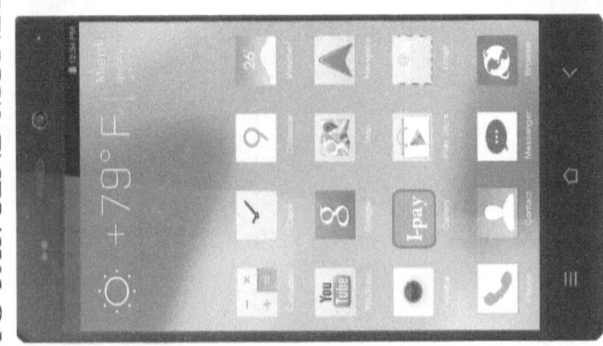

Select App by touching I-pay icon on screen to launch and transact

Touch Pay/Send button to send money to anyone....

Enter payee details by typing or scan QR code by selecting to open camera and point towards the card to capture payee details. Amount, purpose Mpin

After selecting Pay/Send button, transaction details should pop out with account balance. And extra layer of protection may be used when amount beyond 10000 intended to transfer like OTP, in-built fingerprint scanner of smart phone and Hug Transaction Password(HTP) if amount is hug.

Annexure: One India One Currency One Payment System (IPay)

TABLET-PC BASED IPAY (M)
MERCHANT APPLICATION

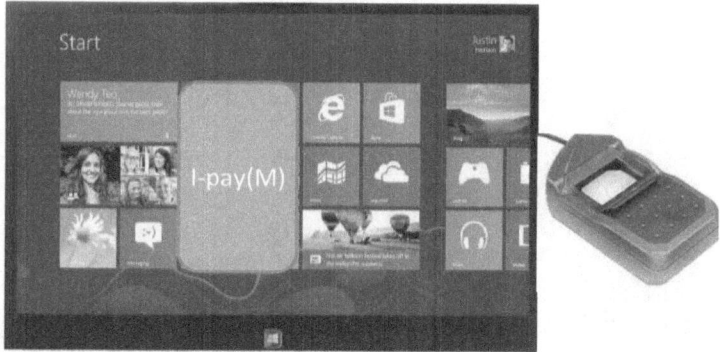

CONDITIONS

- IPay Merchant Module (on Tablet-PC), which works as the retail accounting and POS simultaneously.

- This can be connected to the printer/third party app for the detailed print of sale and payment receipt on single page.

- When the customer pays the bill, this app scan the massage and update the bills as payment received and sends for the bill print/save.

- This works with both USSD and Internet channel for POS functioning. Accepting payment. However, limited functions only possible with USSD channel as it lacks built-in support for larger data communication. Therefore, extra layer of authentication, finger print scanner can not be implemented which is mandatory for high volume transactions.

- *Merchant ID/terminal ID,* this is generated against each Tablet PC whenever any merchant registered the device with the Ipay (M). This ID is seeded to to merchant saving/current account. Whenever any customer want to pay for merchandise bill he needs to enter this *Merchant Id* at payee field. You may wonder why this is required. Right! This facilitates the merchant easy accounting and transaction tracking.

- Fingerprint scanner, you may be in doubt, how the scanner is included when he is against the concept of AADHAAR based transaction. Here one to note that fingerprint can only be accessed as aadhaar is linked. However, system does not allows the Aadhaar Numer as the account number or as user ID.

- It offers great flexibility and cost effectiveness for the merchant.

MERCHANT PAYMENT SYSTEM WITH IPAY (M).................ON TABLET PC

Select I-Pay icon or long press rupees symbol on the Indian keyboard to launch merchant I-pay point of payments (POP) software in TAB or Large Screen Smart Phone.(which need to be registered

Whenever customer pays bills they ques up instantly for acceptance/decline from merchant. On acceptance balance is updated and receipt is printed.

Here RADHIKA customer paid and ques up but merchant not approved and sent for print.

Whenever customer not in the possession of mobile to pay bills, merchant simply click on REQUEST PAYMENT tab and ask customer to enter the necessary details/scan QR code if customer having smart wallet card and authenticate with fingerprint scanner and MPIN according to volume of bill. (for high volume both authentic methods are required)

SL. NO	PAYER DETAILS	AMT	Dr/Cr	PURPOSE	TOTBAL	STATUS
01	SIVA xxxxxxx	30.30	Cr	MILKPACK	3200.30	DONE
02	RADHIKA xxxxx	380.00	Cr	GROERIE		ACCEPT/DECLINE
03	SATHISH xxxxx	490.00	Cr	PULSES	3690.30	DONE
04	GANESH xxxxxx	20	Dr	ITEM RETURN	3670.30	DONE

I-PAY MERCHANT ID XXXX XXXX XXXX

PAY	MERCHANT	REQUEST PAYMENT	
SALE	STATEMENT	SCAN FOR PAYMENTS	EXIT

IPAY WALLET CARD

CONDITIONS AND OUTLINES

- This is introduced to replace the child pocket wallets.
- More control on the children spending. Presently parents should deposit money to their bank account or give away hard cash if they are not eligible to open the bank account. In both cases they do not have the control over their child expenses.
- This is also vary useful when individual not in possession of mobile and want to use for payments in both conventional method at POS and new method of IPay.
- This is linked to the both the parent account and child Aadhaar number. This makes ease of transaction tracking by parents and authority.
- These cards can be topped up, suspended etc. Even this card transactions can be programmed by the parents through IPay App in the aspect of the limit of single transaction and other restrictions. Which ensures complete monitoring and control over the child. Specimen screen shots are provided in following pages for your reference.
- This card automatically ceases to work as and when child becomes the matured individual by gaining the age of the 18 years. In such a cases, he can have the individual bank account.

Annexure: One India One Currency One Payment System (IPay)

CARD CHARACTERISTICS

This QR picture can be scanned by any merchant/individual smart phone for capturing account number so as to reduce the transaction time

This chip serves as same as currently doing with debit card/credit card at POS at different stores

On reverse side, Photo of child and signature are available.

TO MANAGE CHILD WALLET CARDS.... TOP UP/SUSPEND..... WITH SMART PHONE...

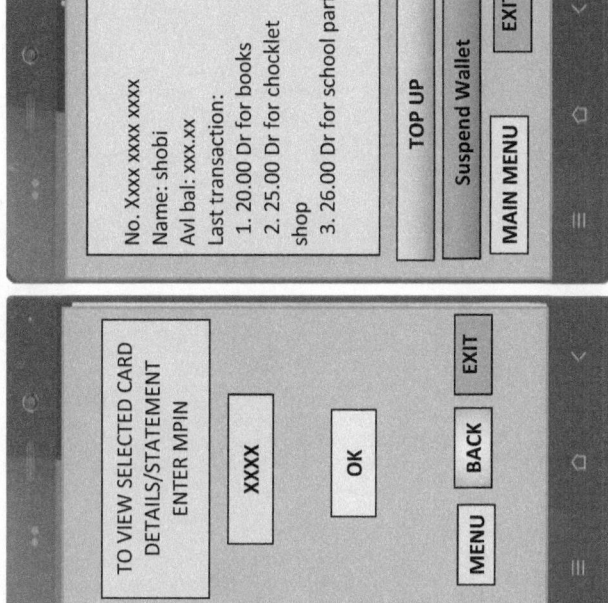

| No. Xxxx xxxx xxxx |
| Name: shobi |
| Avl bal : xxx.xx |
| Last transaction: |
| 1. 20.00 Dr for books |
| 2. 25.00 Dr for chocklet shop |
| 3. 26.00 Dr for school party |

| TOP UP |
| Suspend Wallet |
| MAIN MENU | EXIT |

After necessary AUTHENDTICATION, massage should pop out presenting card details with past transaction etc.......with option shown above.

| TO VIEW SELECTED CARD DETAILS/STATEMENT ENTER MPIN |
| xxxx |
| OK |
| MENU | BACK | EXIT |

Enter MPIN or scan finger at inbuilt finger print scanner for authentication of transaction.......

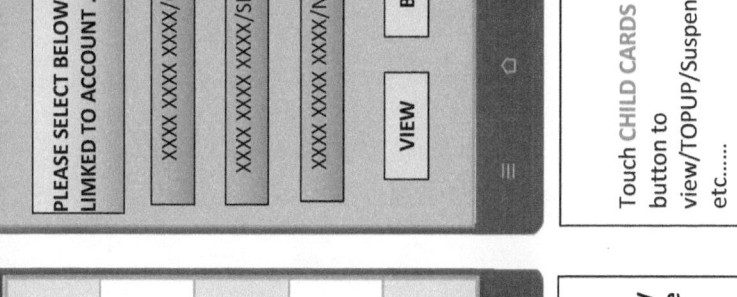

| PLEASE SELECT BELOW CARDS LIMKED TO ACCOUNT ..... |
| XXXX XXXX XXXX/GAI |
| XXXX XXXX XXXX/SHOBI |
| XXXX XXXX XXXX/NIHAL |
| VIEW | BACK |

Touch CHILD CARDS button to view/TOPUP/Suspend etc......

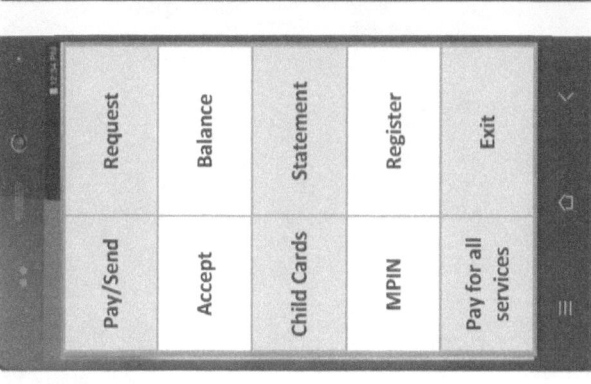

Pay/Send	Request
Accept	Balance
Child Cards	Statement
MPIN	Register
Pay for all services	Exit

Select app by touching I-pay icon on screen to get the main menu screen.....

Bibliography

Economic survey 2015–16, 16–17. Union budget of India: 2017 (Finance Minister Speech and other Articles). Various national and regional news articles along with various official websites of Government Ministries and other Independent departments are also referenced. Few of key websites are listed below.

- *www.mygov.in*
- *www.en.wikipedia.org*
- *www.narendramodi.in*
- *www.niti.gov.in/*
- *www.rbi.org.in*
- *www.uidai.gov.in*
- *www.google.com*
- *www.mospi.gov.in*
- *www.mospi.nic.in*
- *www.finmin.nic.in*
- *www.indiabudget.nic.in*
- *www.agriculture.gov.in*
- *www.socialjustice.nic.in*
- *www.disabilityaffairs.gov.in*

www.ingramcontent.com/pod-product-compliance
Lightning Source LLC
Chambersburg PA
CBHW020425220526
45464CB00002B/575